**Cambridge School
Shakespeare**

MACBETH

Edited by Linzy Brady and David James
Series editors: Richard Andrews and Vicki Wienand
Founding editor: Rex Gibson

CAMBRIDGE
UNIVERSITY PRESS

CAMBRIDGE
UNIVERSITY PRESS

University Printing House, Cambridge CB2 8BS, United Kingdom

One Liberty Plaza, 20th Floor, New York, NY 10006, USA

477 Williamstown Road, Port Melbourne, VIC 3207, Australia

4843/24, 2nd Floor, Ansari Road, Daryaganj, Delhi – 110002, India

79 Anson Road, #06–04/06, Singapore 079906

Cambridge University Press is part of the University of Cambridge.

It furthers the University's mission by disseminating knowledge in the pursuit of education, learning and research at the highest international levels of excellence.

www.cambridge.org
Information on this title: www.cambridge.org/9781107615496

First published 1993
Second edition 2005
Third edition 2014
20 19 18

Printed in Italy by Rotolito S.p.A.

A catalogue record for this publication is available from the British Library

ISBN 978-1-107-61549-6 Paperback

Contents

Introduction

This *Macbeth* is part of the **Cambridge School Shakespeare** series. Like every other play in the series, it has been specially prepared to help all students in schools and colleges.

The **Cambridge School Shakespeare** *Macbeth* aims to be different. It invites you to lift the words from the page and to bring the play to life in your classroom, hall or drama studio. Through enjoyable and focused activities, you will increase your understanding of the play. Actors have created their different interpretations of the play over the centuries. Similarly, you are invited to make up your own mind about *Macbeth*, rather than having someone else's interpretation handed down to you.

Cambridge School Shakespeare does not offer you a cut-down or simplified version of the play. This is Shakespeare's language, filled with imaginative possibilities. You will find on every left-hand page: a summary of the action, an explanation of unfamiliar words, and a choice of activities on Shakespeare's stagecraft, characters, themes and language.

Between each act and in the pages at the end of the play, you will find notes, illustrations and activities. These will help to encourage reflection after every act, and give you insights into the background and context of the play as a whole.

This edition will be of value to you whether you are studying for an examination, reading for pleasure or thinking of putting on the play to entertain others. You can work on the activities on your own or in groups. Many of the activities suggest a particular group size, but don't be afraid to make up larger or smaller groups to suit your own purposes. Please don't think you have to do every activity: choose those that will help you most.

Although you are invited to treat *Macbeth* as a play, you don't need special dramatic or theatrical skills to do the activities. By choosing your activities, and by exploring and experimenting, you can make your own interpretations of Shakespeare's language, characters and stories.

Whatever you do, remember that Shakespeare wrote his plays to be acted, watched and enjoyed.

Rex Gibson
Founding editor

This new edition contains more photographs, more diversity and more supporting material than previous editions, whilst remaining true to Rex's original vision. Specifically, it contains more activities and commentary on stagecraft and writing about Shakespeare, to reflect contemporary interest. The glossary has been enlarged too. Finally, this edition aims to reflect the best teaching and learning possible, and to represent not only Shakespeare through the ages, but also the relevance and excitement of Shakespeare today.

Richard Andrews and Vicki Wienand
Series editors

This edition of *Macbeth* uses the text of the play established by A. R. Braunmuller in **The New Cambridge Shakespeare**.

Macbeth dramatises the story of a brave soldier who is tempted by witches and urged by his wife to murder his way to the throne of Scotland. It is a play about ambition, murder, intrigue, manipulation, seduction and betrayal.

Three Witches make prophecies about Macbeth's future and tempt him to murder. The Witches have been portrayed in very different ways on stage: as supernatural harbingers of chaos; as instruments of evil to tempt Macbeth to destruction; as figures of destiny or fate; and as figments of Macbeth's overwrought imagination. You can find other pictures of the Witches on pages 8, 10, 37 and 131.

Shakespeare gives the Witches a style of speaking all their own, a rhythmic language of charms and curses, to emphasise the theme of magic and the supernatural in the play.

What is the relationship between Macbeth and his wife? Although she dominates him in the first two acts, many productions show a loving relationship between them.

The complex relationship between Macbeth and Lady Macbeth develops rapidly over the course of the play. Their interdependence is complicated by manipulation, murder and an increasing alienation from each other. You can find other portrayals of the Macbeths on pages 44, 74, 86, 97, 166, 171, 177 and 178.

Macbeth and Lady Macbeth are partners in crime. Although Lady Macbeth could not kill King Duncan as he slept because he reminded her of her father, she takes charge once Macbeth has committed the murder. She carries the bloodstained daggers back into the room, frames the guards by smearing blood on them, and tells Macbeth that a 'little water clears us of this deed'. The murder of Duncan is a turning point in the play.

For much of the play, Lady Macbeth seems a stronger character than Macbeth himself, overturning traditional ideas of masculinity and femininity.

After Duncan's murder, Macbeth and Lady Macbeth become king and queen. They maintain an innocent appearance of grief and modesty to hide their evil deeds and ambitious desires. This 'false face' is only threatened in the famous banquet scene, as Macbeth reacts violently to the sight of Banquo's ghost while Lady Macbeth tries to keep up appearances (shown here in a Taiwanese adaptation of the play).

As something of a contrast to the dark atmosphere of the play, the Porter provides some comic relief in Act 2 Scene 3. The Porter's joke about 'an equivocator' (someone who does not tell the truth) echoes the theme of deception and the conflict between appearance and reality that runs through the play.

Lady Macbeth is increasingly consumed by guilt and alienated from Macbeth as he tries to shield her from more murder. Lady Macbeth's repression of this guilt leads to self-destructive behaviour and mental instability. At the end of the play, we see her walking in her sleep, in terror of darkness, obsessively washing her hands and ultimately suicidal.

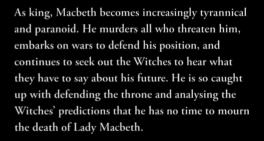

As king, Macbeth becomes increasingly tyrannical and paranoid. He murders all who threaten him, embarks on wars to defend his position, and continues to seek out the Witches to hear what they have to say about his future. He is so caught up with defending the throne and analysing the Witches' predictions that he has no time to mourn the death of Lady Macbeth.

▶ In Act 5 Scene 8, Macduff confronts Macbeth, the man responsible for the murder of his family. Macbeth realises that the Witches have misled him and falsely promised safety in battle. Despite this, he fights on – choosing death over the humiliation of being paraded like a 'baited bear in front of the rabble'.

▼ In the final speech of the play, Malcolm, son of Duncan, becomes king and grants earldoms to Macduff and the other thanes. Although order has been restored after Macbeth's death, the audience is left to wonder if peace has really returned to Scotland.

List of characters

The Royal House of Scotland

DUNCAN King of Scotland
MALCOLM his elder son
DONALDBAIN his younger son

Thanes (noblemen of Scotland), their households and supporters

MACBETH Thane of Glamis
    later Thane of Cawdor
    later King of Scotland
LADY MACBETH
BANQUO
FLEANCE Banquo's son
MACDUFF Thane of Fife
LADY MACDUFF
SON OF MACDUFF
GENTLEWOMAN Lady Macbeth's attendant
SEYTON Macbeth's armour bearer
PORTER at Macbeth's castle
CAPTAIN wounded in battle

AN OLD MAN	ROSS
DOCTOR of physic	LENNOX
FIRST MURDERER	MENTEITH
SECOND MURDERER	ANGUS
THIRD MURDERER	CAITHNESS

} other thanes

The supernatural world

THREE WITCHES the weird sisters
THREE APPARITIONS
HECATE Queen of Witchcraft
THREE OTHER WITCHES

The English

SIWARD Earl of Northumberland
YOUNG SIWARD his son
ENGLISH DOCTOR at the court of King Edward the Confessor

Lords, Soldiers, Attendants, Servants, Messengers

The play is set in Scotland and England

Stagecraft

Dramatic entrance (in small groups, then by yourself)

Shakespeare makes *Macbeth* literally start with a bang. The Witches enter the scene with a clap of thunder, which in Shakespeare's day may have been created backstage by rolling a cannonball across wooden boards.

a Look at the photographs of modern productions in the 'Looking back' section on page 37, then talk about how you would stage this opening scene in your own modern production. How do the Witches look and sound? How do they move, enter and exit? What sound effects might add to the menacing mood? How would you heighten the dramatic effect of this scene?

b In role as the director of a new modern production of *Macbeth*, write a letter to a close friend describing your ideas for staging this scene.

Write about it

Confusion and ambiguity (in threes)

Read Scene 1 aloud with two other people. Try to explain to one another what each line means. If the meaning of any lines is obscure, consider why Shakespeare may have written those lines so they were deliberately confusing. After the discussion, write a paragraph that explains how Shakespeare uses ambiguity and contradiction to heighten the dramatic interest of the scene.

1 Diabolic language (whole class, then by yourself)

a Identify the Witches' use of rhythm and rhyme. Saying the words out loud should help you hear a beat that creates a chant-like rhythm (DUM da DUM da DUM da DUM). This rhythm is called trochaic tetrameter. While reading the lines out loud, shift your weight (or walk slowly round the classroom) in time to the beat. If you find this difficult, clap your hands at each stressed syllable to find the beat.

b In lines 1–7, the Witches speak in short, rhythmic lines, and this scene finishes with a couplet (two lines that end in the same rhyme). Make up your own rhyming couplet for Hecate, a fourth witch who joins these three later in the play.

hurly-burly fighting, confusion

ere before

heath wilderness

I come the Witches address their familiar spirits ('familiars'): demons who helped with their evil work and usually took the form of animals
Graymalkin grey cat
Paddock toad

Alarum trumpet call to battle or to warn of danger
within off stage

plight unfortunate condition
newest state latest situation
sergeant a soldier who, at the time, could be the equivalent of a captain
hardy brave
fought … captivity rescued me from capture

Macbeth

Act 1 Scene 1
A desolate place

Thunder and lightning. Enter three WITCHES

FIRST WITCH   When shall we three meet again?
                In thunder, lightning, or in rain?
SECOND WITCH   When the hurly-burly's done,
                When the battle's lost, and won.   *[when the battle is done and won]*
THIRD WITCH   That will be ere the set of sun.   5
FIRST WITCH   Where the place?
SECOND WITCH   Upon the heath.
THIRD WITCH   There to meet with Macbeth.
FIRST WITCH   I come, Graymalkin.
SECOND WITCH   Paddock calls.   10
THIRD WITCH   Anon.
ALL   Fair is foul, and foul is fair,
                Hover through the fog and filthy air.

                                                        Exeunt

Act 1 Scene 2
King Duncan's camp near Forres

Alarum within. Enter King [DUNCAN,] MALCOLM, DONALD-
BAIN, LENNOX, *with Attendants, meeting a bleeding* CAPTAIN

DUNCAN   What bloody man is that? He can report,
           As seemeth by his plight, of the revolt
           The newest state.
MALCOLM   This is the sergeant
           Who like a good and hardy soldier fought
           'Gainst my captivity. Hail, brave friend;   5

The wounded Captain reports that although the rebel Macdonald had strong forces, Macbeth personally killed him. Facing an assault by fresh Norwegian troops, Macbeth and Banquo fought on undaunted.

Language in the play
The Captain's report (by yourself)

The Captain's words are carefully chosen to capture the battle and paint a picture for his onstage audience (Duncan and the noblemen), as well as for the audience in the theatre.

Read lines 16–23 aloud. Identify four visual images that help the audience picture key moments in the battle. For example, you might want to look for images that depict Macbeth in the fray ('his brandished steel, / Which smoked with bloody execution') or when he meets his enemy ('And fixed his head upon our battlements'). When you have selected your four visual images, draw them or write a short paragraph for each one describing the impact it has.

Write about it
First impressions (by yourself, then in pairs)

a   Imagine you fought in the battle that the Captain describes. Using details from the script opposite, write a diary entry at the end of the day describing your impression of Macbeth. How would you turn some of the visual images into a straightforward eye-witness account?

b   Swap your piece of writing with a classmate. Read each other's entries and then talk together about the difference Shakespeare's language makes in evoking the battle. How do the visual images created by the Captain's words have a different impact from the narrative details in your own account of the battle? (For example, look at descriptions such as 'two spent swimmers that do cling together' or 'cannons over-charged with double cracks'.)

1 The wounded Captain writes home

Imagine you are the wounded Captain. You have had your wounds dressed and now you write home to tell your family what has happened. Base your letter on lines 7–42.

---

broil battle

choke their art when two swimmers try to cling to each other, they stop each other from swimming and both drown

for to that to that end

kerns lightly armed soldiers who often used a sword or bow and arrows

galloglasses heavily armed soldiers often carrying a heavy battle axe

Fortune fickle luck

Valour's minion bravery's favourite

carved out his passage sliced his way

unseamed him ripped him open

nave to th'chaps navel to the jaws

'gins his reflection begins to fade

direful dreadful, terrible

Mark pay attention

skipping leaping in fright

trust their heels run away

surveying vantage seeing an opportunity

furbished polished, cleaned

say sooth speak the truth

cracks cannon shots

doubly redoubled eightfold blows

reeking streaming with blood

memorise another Golgotha re-enact a slaughter like Christ's crucifixion

Say to the king the knowledge of the broil
As thou didst leave it.

CAPTAIN   Doubtful it stood,
As two spent swimmers that do cling together
And choke their art. The merciless Macdonald –
Worthy to be a rebel, for to that   10
The multiplying villainies of nature
Do swarm upon him – from the Western Isles
Of kerns and galloglasses is supplied,
And Fortune on his damnèd quarrel smiling,
Showed like a rebel's whore. But all's too weak,   15
For brave Macbeth – well he deserves that name –
Disdaining Fortune, with his brandished steel,
Which smoked with bloody execution,
Like Valour's minion carved out his passage
Till he faced the slave,   20
Which ne'er shook hands, nor bade farewell to him,
Till he unseamed him from the nave to th'chaps
And fixed his head upon our battlements.

DUNCAN   O valiant cousin, worthy gentleman.

CAPTAIN   As whence the sun 'gins his reflection,   25
Shipwrecking storms and direful thunders,
So from that spring whence comfort seemed to come,
Discomfort swells. Mark, King of Scotland, mark,
No sooner justice had, with valour armed,
Compelled these skipping kerns to trust their heels,   30
But the Norwegian lord, surveying vantage,
With furbished arms and new supplies of men
Began a fresh assault.

DUNCAN   Dismayed not this our captains, Macbeth and Banquo?

CAPTAIN   Yes, as sparrows, eagles, or the hare, the lion.   35
If I say sooth, I must report they were
As cannons over-charged with double cracks;
So they doubly redoubled strokes upon the foe.
Except they meant to bathe in reeking wounds
Or memorise another Golgotha,   40
I cannot tell.
But I am faint, my gashes cry for help.

[handwritten annotation:] redoubled their efforts and ne pushed them back

Ross tells that Macbeth has triumphed, capturing Cawdor and obtaining ransom and a favourable peace treaty from the King of Norway. Duncan sentences Cawdor to death and confers his title on Macbeth.

1 What is Macbeth like? (in small groups)

In your groups, talk about and then draw up a list of the qualities you think Macbeth possesses. Include some quotations from the play so far. Present a tableau (a 'human sculpture', like a still photograph) that shows Macbeth as he has been described up to this point in the play. Your tableau might represent a moment in the battle or it could be a more symbolic depiction of Macbeth's qualities.

Language in the play

What is Duncan like? (in pairs)

Duncan's language is formal and his vocabulary ('honour', 'worthy', 'noble') associates him with qualities that are both admirable and kingly. With a partner, discuss how you would advise an actor playing Duncan to speak his lines in this scene. How would they contrast with the speeches made by the other characters? After the discussion, read those lines out loud in the style you have decided on.

▼ Macbeth's world is brutal and violent. How do scenes like the one pictured here create a specific ideal of masculinity?

smack taste, savour

Thane head of a clan in Scotland
looks is visible

flout mock, jeer

Bellona Roman goddess of war
bridegroom Macbeth, who has become married to the cause of war
lapped in proof clad in armour
self-comparisons similar actions
Point against point sword to sword
Curbing restraining, constraining
lavish unrestrained or impetuous
composition a peace treaty
deign permit
Saint Colm's Inch Isle of Incholm (see map, p. 60)
dollars English word for the German thaler, a large silver coin
bosom interest heartfelt concerns
present immediate
former title Thane of Cawdor

DUNCAN   So well thy words become thee as thy wounds;
They smack of honour both. Go get him surgeons.

               [Exit Captain, attended]

       Enter ROSS *and* ANGUS

Who comes here?

MALCOLM   The worthy Thane of Ross.   45

LENNOX   What a haste looks through his eyes! So should he look
That seems to speak things strange.

ROSS   God save the king.

DUNCAN   Whence cam'st thou, worthy thane?

ROSS   From Fife, great king,
Where the Norwegian banners flout the sky
And fan our people cold.   *They won the war*   50
Norway himself, with terrible numbers,   *They alowd them to*
Assisted by that most disloyal traitor,   *bury their dead and*
The Thane of Cawdor, began a dismal conflict,   *took their reparations*
Till that Bellona's bridegroom, lapped in proof,
Confronted him with self-comparisons,   55
Point against point, rebellious arm 'gainst arm,
Curbing his lavish spirit. And to conclude,
The victory fell on us –

DUNCAN   Great happiness! –

ROSS   That now Sweno,
The Norways' king, craves composition.
Nor would we deign him burial of his men   60
Till he disbursèd at Saint Colm's Inch
Ten thousand dollars to our general use.   *want him killed*

DUNCAN   No more that Thane of Cawdor shall deceive
Our bosom interest. Go pronounce his present death
And with his former title greet Macbeth.   65

ROSS   I'll see it done.

DUNCAN   What he hath lost, noble Macbeth hath won.

                  Exeunt

The Witches await Macbeth. They plot to torment a sea captain whose wife has insulted them. A drum signals the approach of Macbeth.

1 Historical witches (in pairs)

a The First Witch is angry with a sailor's wife who would not give her some chestnuts. The wife's response gives us some insights into the way witches were viewed in Shakespeare's day. With a partner, discuss what this passage tells us about the Witches and their supposed powers over both people and nature.

b Look at the images below of witches as they have been represented historically, and identify the witch-like qualities depicted there. Then read the script opposite and add to your list.

c How do the qualities on your list differ from depictions of witches and other supernatural characters in popular movies and books today? Describe these differences in a letter to a younger student interested in contemporary representations of the supernatural.

Language in the play
Metaphor for life (in pairs)

The image of a ship tossed by the winds and the waves, struggling to make it to a safe harbour, has often been used as a **metaphor** for life. Life is seen as a voyage during which we face difficulties, experience adventures and make discoveries. Discuss the impact the Witches have on the 'voyage' of the sailor in the script opposite. What does this metaphor reveal about the Witches' plans to meet with Macbeth?

quoth said

Aroint thee clear off

rump-fed well-fed, selfish, indulgent

runnion general term of abuse, especially for a woman

Aleppo trading city in northern Syria, which was part of the Turkish Empire

Tiger in 1606 an English ship called the *Tiger* finally arrived home after a disastrous voyage lasting 567 days (81 weeks)

sieve sailing in sieves was thought to be a common practice among witches

wind witches were imagined to control the wind

very ports they blow winds prevent ships from entering every port

quarters geographical directions

card compass

penthouse lid eyelid

forbid cursed

sennights weeks (one sennight is seven days)

nine times nine 9 weeks × 9 weeks = 81 weeks

peak, and pine waste away

bark small ship

pilot guide who steers ships to harbour

Act 1 Scene 3
A heath

Thunder. Enter the three WITCHES

FIRST WITCH	Where hast thou been, sister?
SECOND WITCH	Killing swine.
THIRD WITCH	Sister, where thou?
FIRST WITCH	A sailor's wife had chestnuts in her lap

[handwritten: went out and messed with a sailor and his wife]

And munched, and munched, and munched. 'Give me', quoth I.
'Aroint thee, witch', the rump-fed runnion cries.   5
Her husband's to Aleppo gone, master o'th'Tiger:
But in a sieve I'll thither sail,
And like a rat without a tail,
I'll do, I'll do, and I'll do.

SECOND WITCH   I'll give thee a wind.   10
FIRST WITCH   Thou'rt kind.
THIRD WITCH   And I another.
FIRST WITCH   I myself have all the other,
And the very ports they blow,
All the quarters that they know   15
I'th'shipman's card.
I'll drain him dry as hay:
Sleep shall neither night nor day
Hang upon his penthouse lid;
He shall live a man forbid.   20
Weary sennights nine times nine,
Shall he dwindle, peak, and pine.
Though his bark cannot be lost,
Yet it shall be tempest-tossed.
Look what I have.
SECOND WITCH   Show me, show me.   25
FIRST WITCH   Here I have a pilot's thumb,
Wrecked as homeward he did come.
Drum within
THIRD WITCH   A drum, a drum;
Macbeth doth come.

The Witches chant a spell to prepare for their meeting with Macbeth. They amaze him with predictions that he will be Thane of Cawdor and King of Scotland. Banquo demands to know his own future.

Stagecraft

A charmed space (in small groups)

The Witches wind up a charm immediately before Macbeth and Banquo enter the scene. Read lines 30–5 with your group.

a The rhythmic, chant-like language of the Witches gives clues about their movements on stage, such as what they are doing when creating the charm, when they speed up and when they stop. In your groups, talk about how you would stage this part of the scene so that you can show Macbeth and Banquo walking into this 'charmed' space.

b Prepare a dramatised reading of the whole passage opposite. Look at Banquo's speech in lines 37–45 for more clues about what is happening on stage.

▼ 'Speak if you can', Macbeth demands. Speak the Witches' predictions in lines 46–8 as you think they would deliver them.

weïrd sisters in Anglo-Saxon mythology, 'Wyrd' (Fate) was a goddess who controlled destiny

Posters speedy travellers

Thrice to thine … to mine three times in your direction and in mine (the Witches perform a dance or use gestures that bind each individual to the group)

nine an action is repeated three times for each Witch

charm spell

wound up placed in readiness

foul and fair the weather is bad, but the outcome of the battle is good

Forres see map, p. 60

aught anything

choppy chapped and cracked by the weather

Glamis (pronounced 'Glahms')

start flinch or make a nervous gesture

fantastical imaginary

present grace immediate favour
noble having new titles of nobility
rapt spellbound, entranced
seeds of time future

ALL	The weïrd sisters, hand in hand,	30
	Posters of the sea and land,	
	Thus do go, about, about,	
	Thrice to thine, and thrice to mine,	
	And thrice again, to make up nine.	
	Peace, the charm's wound up.	35

→ 3 = magic number (handwritten note)

Enter MACBETH *and* BANQUO

MACBETH	So foul and fair a day I have not seen.	
BANQUO	How far is't called to Forres? What are these,	
	So withered and so wild in their attire,	
	That look not like th'inhabitants o'th'earth,	
	And yet are on't? – Live you, or are you aught	40
	That man may question? You seem to understand me,	
	By each at once her choppy finger laying	
	Upon her skinny lips; you should be women,	
	And yet your beards forbid me to interpret	
	That you are so.	
MACBETH	Speak if you can: what are you?	45
FIRST WITCH	All hail Macbeth, hail to thee, Thane of Glamis.	
SECOND WITCH	All hail Macbeth, hail to thee, Thane of Cawdor.	
THIRD WITCH	All hail Macbeth, that shalt be king hereafter.	

→ means his uncle has to die – Duncan (handwritten note)

BANQUO	Good sir, why do you start and seem to fear	
	Things that do sound so fair? – I'th'name of truth	50
	Are ye fantastical, or that indeed	
	Which outwardly ye show? My noble partner	
	You greet with present grace and great prediction	
	Of noble having and of royal hope	
	That he seems rapt withal. To me you speak not.	55
	If you can look into the seeds of time	
	And say which grain will grow and which will not,	
	Speak then to me, who neither beg nor fear	
	Your favours nor your hate.	
FIRST WITCH	Hail.	60
SECOND WITCH	Hail.	
THIRD WITCH	Hail.	

The Witches prophesy that Banquo's descendants will be kings, but he himself will not. Refusing to answer Macbeth's questions, the Witches vanish. Ross brings news of Duncan's delight at Macbeth's victory.

Stagecraft

How do the Witches vanish?

Every director of the play has to solve the practical problem of the stage direction 'Witches vanish'. At the beginning of Roman Polanski's movie version, the Witches vanished by walking away from the camera along a dismal beach, fading into specks that dissolved into the opening credits. On Shakespeare's stage there were obvious limitations to the way the Witches could vanish. They may have left on foot or via a trapdoor, or have somehow 'flown' off stage.

Write out your own suggestions for making the Witches vanish convincingly in a letter to a director working on a production in a modern theatre, which will later be turned into a film.

Characters

To be 'rapt withal' (in pairs)

Macbeth and Banquo are 'rapt withal' by the Witches' prophecies. Read the scene again, from their entrance after line 35, then write out five questions for these two characters. Step into role as either Macbeth or Banquo and answer your partner's questions.

1 Actors' experiments (in pairs)

Imagine you are an actor in rehearsal, taking advice from a director who wants to experiment with different ways of representing the scene opposite. Read the director's instructions below:

- In lines 68–76, Macbeth just can't believe what he has heard. He wants answers urgently. So speak the lines quickly and angrily *or* in a way that shows he is confused and frustrated.
- In lines 77–86, the two men are deeply puzzled and amazed by what they have seen and heard. So speak the lines slowly and wonderingly *or* fearfully and suspiciously.
- In lines 87–98, Ross wants to give Macbeth and Banquo important news from the king. So speak the lines pompously and grandly *or* with friendliness and excitement.

Choose how you want to interpret these lines, then take turns to perform your version of this scene to the rest of the class.

---

get be father of

Finel Macbeth's father

Stands not ... belief is unbelievable

intelligence news, information

charge command, order

corporal physical

on of
the insane root hemlock, henbane or deadly nightshade (when eaten, it produces madness)

selfsame tune identical meaning

reads understands

stout brave, valiant
Nothing afeard not afraid

post with post many messages

FIRST WITCH	Lesser than Macbeth, and greater.
SECOND WITCH	Not so happy, yet much happier.
THIRD WITCH	Thou shalt get kings, though thou be none.

THIRD WITCH   Thou shalt get kings, though thou be none.   65
           So all hail Macbeth and Banquo.

FIRST WITCH   Banquo and Macbeth, all hail.

MACBETH   Stay, you imperfect speakers. Tell me more.
By Finel's death, I know I am Thane of Glamis,
But how of Cawdor? The Thane of Cawdor lives   70
A prosperous gentleman, and to be king
Stands not within the prospect of belief,
No more than to be Cawdor. Say from whence
You owe this strange intelligence, or why
Upon this blasted heath you stop our way   75
With such prophetic greeting? Speak, I charge you.

Witches vanish

BANQUO   The earth hath bubbles, as the water has,
And these are of them. Whither are they vanished?

MACBETH   Into the air, and what seemed corporal,
Melted, as breath into the wind. Would they had stayed.   80

BANQUO   Were such things here as we do speak about?
Or have we eaten on the insane root,
That takes the reason prisoner?

MACBETH   Your children shall be kings.

BANQUO   You shall be king.

MACBETH   And Thane of Cawdor too: went it not so?   85

BANQUO   To th'selfsame tune and words – who's here?

Enter ROSS *and* ANGUS

ROSS   The king hath happily received, Macbeth,
The news of thy success, and when he reads
Thy personal venture in the rebels' sight,
His wonders and his praises do contend   90
Which should be thine or his. Silenced with that,
In viewing o'er the rest o'th'selfsame day,
He finds thee in the stout Norwegian ranks,
Nothing afeard of what thyself didst make,
Strange images of death. As thick as tale   95
Came post with post, and every one did bear
Thy praises in his kingdom's great defence,
And poured them down before him.

Macbeth is amazed to hear that he is now Thane of Cawdor. Angus explains that the treacherous thane has been sentenced to death. Banquo warns that the Witches' predictions might lead to evil.

Themes

Honour and kingship

Angus tells that the present Thane of Cawdor is alive, but has committed treason and sided with the enemy. Use lines 107–15 to help you write the official notice that gives reasons for Cawdor's conviction for treason and announces his imminent execution. You may find it helpful to start by considering the themes and ideas of kingship, honour and masculinity that are raised here, perhaps in the form of a mind map or as bullet points.

1 Secret desires (in pairs)

Macbeth and Banquo are comrades in arms, who have fought together and won a great victory. But how might the Witches' prophecies affect them and their relationship?

a With a partner, read out Macbeth's and Banquo's lines opposite. Talk together about the meaning of Banquo's words in lines 121–5 in relation to the theme of appearance versus reality. (See p. 161 for more information on this theme.) What do you think counts as 'reality' here?

b Imagine that Shakespeare left some space for another aside at the end of this exchange. What thoughts or feelings would your character hide from his comrade in arms? In role as either Macbeth or Banquo, speak out your secret thoughts about the Witches and each other. Write out these thoughts in **blank verse** (see p. 172), modelled on the speeches Shakespeare has given the characters in this scene.

earnest promise, pledge

addition new title

Who he who
heavy judgement death sentence

line reinforce
vantage additional amount of soldiers, weapons, money
wrack ruin or overthrow
capital mortal or meriting death

The greatest the larger part of the prophecy
behind in the past

home fully or to the end
enkindle inflame with desire

instruments of darkness devils (the Witches)
Win us … consequence tell us the truth about small matters, but lie about matters that have grave consequences
Cousins kinsmen

ANGUS	We are sent	
	To give thee from our royal master thanks;	
	Only to herald thee into his sight,	100
	Not pay thee.	
ROSS	And for an earnest of a greater honour,	
	He bade me, from him, call thee Thane of Cawdor:	
	In which addition, hail most worthy thane,	
	For it is thine.	
BANQUO	What, can the devil speak true?	105
MACBETH	The Thane of Cawdor lives. Why do you dress me	
	In borrowed robes?	
ANGUS	Who was the thane, lives yet,	
	But under heavy judgement bears that life	
	Which he deserves to lose.	
	Whether he was combined with those of Norway,	110
	Or did line the rebel with hidden help	
	And vantage, or that with both he laboured	
	In his country's wrack, I know not,	
	But treasons capital, confessed and proved,	
	Have overthrown him.	
MACBETH	[*Aside*] Glamis, and Thane of Cawdor:	115
	The greatest is behind. – Thanks for your pains. –	
	[*To Banquo*] Do you not hope your children shall be kings,	
	When those that gave the Thane of Cawdor to me	
	Promised no less to them?	
BANQUO	That trusted home,	
	Might yet enkindle you unto the crown,	120
	Besides the Thane of Cawdor. But 'tis strange,	
	And oftentimes, to win us to our harm,	
	The instruments of darkness tell us truths;	
	Win us with honest trifles, to betray's	
	In deepest consequence. –	125
	Cousins, a word, I pray you.	

Macbeth weighs the moral implications of the Witches' prediction. He is horrified at the thought of killing Duncan, but resolves to accept whatever has to be. He proposes that he and Banquo talk together later.

1 Macbeth's private thoughts (in pairs)

An aside is a dramatic device that gives important insights into a character's thoughts and feelings. In lines 126–43, Macbeth processes the news that he is now the Thane of Cawdor and that one of the Witches' prophecies has come true.

In pairs, one person reads these lines aloud, pausing at every punctuation mark. The other person says 'Hail Macbeth, King of Scotland' in these pauses, either in a tempting voice or echoing the way the Witches might have said it. Work out how many times Macbeth refers to the murder of Duncan. Afterwards, talk together about whether you think this prediction is uppermost in Macbeth's mind each time he speaks.

2 Punctuation clues

Macbeth's confusion is evident in this section, as he wavers between murderous thoughts and an awareness of good and evil. Think about how the language makes you feel as you read the lines opposite while walking round the classroom. As you walk, you should change direction on each punctuation mark, using the following rules:

- At each full stop make a full about-turn (180 degrees).
- At each comma make a half turn (90 degrees to your right or left).

Which words or lines stood out for you during this activity? How did this activity improve your understanding of Macbeth's thoughts and feelings?

Language in the play

Borrowed robes (in pairs)

Earlier in this scene, in lines 106–7, the first of many images of clothing is used. There is also a subtle reference to clothes in line 111, where 'line' also means the lining or reinforcement of a cloak (Cawdor had reinforced the rebel forces).

a Look for imagery relating to clothing in the script opposite. Discuss how this adds depth to the language and links different ideas. Remember that 'rapt' (line 141) means spellbound, but also sounds like 'wrapped', as in 'wrapped up in a new cloak'.

b Start compiling a list of imagery that relates to clothing, and add to this as you read through the rest of the play.

soliciting promising of pleasure

unfix my hair make my hair stand on end

seated fixed in position

use ordinary course or state

Present fears ... imaginings real dangers are less frightening than those I can imagine

function activity or movement

surmise imaginings

strange unfamiliar

cleave cling

Time ... roughest day what will be, will be

favour intelligence

wrought disturbed, agitated

registered ... leaf Macbeth uses the image of a notebook that will help him remember what he owes Ross and Angus

chanced happened

The interim having weighed it after time for thought

free plain-speaking

MACBETH	[*Aside*] Two truths are told,

As happy prologues to the swelling act
Of the imperial theme. – I thank you, gentlemen. –
This supernatural soliciting
Cannot be ill, cannot be good. If ill,   130
Why hath it given me earnest of success,
Commencing in a truth? I am Thane of Cawdor.
If good, why do I yield to that suggestion,
Whose horrid image doth unfix my hair
And make my seated heart knock at my ribs   135
Against the use of nature? Present fears
Are less than horrible imaginings.
My thought, whose murder yet is but fantastical,
Shakes so my single state of man that function
Is smothered in surmise, and nothing is,   140
But what is not.

BANQUO	Look how our partner's rapt.
MACBETH	If chance will have me king, why chance may crown me

Without my stir.

BANQUO	New honours come upon him

Like our strange garments, cleave not to their mould,
But with the aid of use.

MACBETH	Come what come may, 145

Time and the hour runs through the roughest day.

BANQUO	Worthy Macbeth, we stay upon your leisure.
MACBETH	Give me your favour. My dull brain was wrought

With things forgotten. Kind gentlemen, your pains
Are registered where every day I turn   150
The leaf to read them. Let us toward the king.
[*To Banquo*] Think upon what hath chanced and at more time,
The interim having weighed it, let us speak
Our free hearts each to other.

BANQUO	Very gladly.
MACBETH	Till then, enough. – Come, friends. 155

Exeunt

Malcolm reports that the Thane of Cawdor died a repentant and dignified death. Duncan reflects that it is impossible to judge anyone by their outward appearance. He warmly welcomes Macbeth.

Stagecraft

Offstage events (whole class)

Because of the limitations of the Jacobean theatre, important events often took place off stage – such as the battle involving Macbeth and the Norwegian forces, or Cawdor's execution. Today, directors often take the same approach in television programmes and movies.

Do you think offstage battles, executions or other important and dramatic events in a story add to or limit an audience's enjoyment and understanding? Write down your ideas, then report back to the rest of the class. Afterwards, hold a class discussion on the benefits and drawbacks of having some events take place off stage.

Themes

Appearance and reality

Duncan claims that you cannot tell what people are like from their appearance ('There's no art / To find the mind's construction in the face'). Discuss with others in your class how far you think this observation is true. Consider your own experiences. Have you ever been judged by what you look like rather than who you really are? Do you think society today judges people more by their appearance than anything else? If you feel comfortable doing so, share these experiences with your class.

1 Dramatic irony

Dramatic irony occurs when the audience knows something that the characters in the play do not. There is a good example of dramatic irony in the script opposite. Just at the moment when Duncan is saying that he wrongly trusted Cawdor ('He was a gentleman on whom I built / An absolute trust'), the man who is thinking of killing him enters.

Imagine you are a director and write notes to the cast about how you would like this crucial entrance to be played. To what extent do you want the actors to emphasise the use of dramatic irony?

Flourish fanfare of trumpets

in commission responsible

repentance regret
Became dignified
studied rehearsed (an image from the theatre)
owed possessed

before beyond my power to pay you

recompense suitable reward

That the ... mine that I could honour you appropriately

More is thy due ... pay you deserve more than anyone can pay

Act 1 Scene 4
Duncan's palace at Forres

Flourish. Enter King DUNCAN, LENNOX, MALCOLM,
DONALDBAIN, *and Attendants*

DUNCAN   Is execution done on Cawdor, or not
Those in commission yet returned?

MALCOLM   My liege,
They are not yet come back. But I have spoke
With one that saw him die, who did report
That very frankly he confessed his treasons,   5
Implored your highness' pardon, and set forth
A deep repentance. Nothing in his life
Became him like the leaving it. He died
As one that had been studied in his death,
To throw away the dearest thing he owed   10
As 'twere a careless trifle.

DUNCAN   There's no art
To find the mind's construction in the face.
He was a gentleman on whom I built
An absolute trust.

Enter MACBETH, BANQUO, ROSS, *and* ANGUS

              O worthiest cousin,
The sin of my ingratitude even now   15
Was heavy on me. Thou art so far before,
That swiftest wing of recompense is slow
To overtake thee. Would thou hadst less deserved,
That the proportion both of thanks and payment
Might have been mine. Only I have left to say,   20
More is thy due than more than all can pay.

MACBETH   The service and the loyalty I owe,
In doing it, pays itself. Your highness' part

Characters

King and future king (in small groups)

This is an important scene, because we see both Duncan and Macbeth develop as characters.

- Duncan is often portrayed on stage as a gentle, kindly king. The language Shakespeare uses here – of reward and growth – reinforces this idea of a generous ruler. But in his decision to name Malcolm as his successor, Duncan also shows himself to be a clever and ruthless politician.

- In lines 22–7, Macbeth is publicly loyal to his king. In lines 48–53, however, he admits to himself that he must find a way to prevent Malcolm being appointed Duncan's heir. It is important to note that in Scotland at the time, kingship was not automatically inherited. This explains Macbeth's disappointment, especially given the Witches' prophecy.

Experiment with different ways of staging the script opposite to show how the characters of Duncan and Macbeth have changed. Think about how each character reacts as the other is talking. Is Duncan being devious or kind? Is Macbeth justified in his response? Remember to consider characters such as Malcolm and Donaldbain, who do not speak in this section but whose lives will be affected by this exchange. How would you play them?

1 Power relationships (in small groups)

Talk about how the characters in this scene would be depicted in a formal portrait. Then take roles and prepare for a group portrait. A 'portrait painter' should arrange the characters in the most diplomatic way. Remember that to accurately show the status of each group of sitters, they should be positioned so that the most important is nearest the king. How do the figures in the Tudor painting below relate to your arrangement?

hither here

enfold embrace

Wanton ... drops of sorrow unrestrained tears

We will establish ... upon I declare as Scotland's next king

invest endow (and also clothe)

Inverness the location of Macbeth's castle

harbinger messenger (an officer who prepared for a king's visit)

The eye wink at the hand to be unaware of the fatal blow

full so supremely
commendations praises or recommendations

peerless beyond comparison

Is to receive our duties, and our duties
Are to your throne and state, children and servants,   25
Which do but what they should by doing everything
Safe toward your love and honour.

DUNCAN   Welcome hither.
I have begun to plant thee and will labour
To make thee full of growing. Noble Banquo,
That hast no less deserved, nor must be known   30
No less to have done so, let me enfold thee
And hold thee to my heart.

BANQUO   There if I grow,
The harvest is your own.

DUNCAN   My plenteous joys,
Wanton in fullness, seek to hide themselves
In drops of sorrow. Sons, kinsmen, thanes,   35
And you whose places are the nearest, know:
We will establish our estate upon
Our eldest, Malcolm, whom we name hereafter
The Prince of Cumberland, which honour must
Not unaccompanied invest him only,   40
But signs of nobleness like stars shall shine
On all deservers. [*To Macbeth*] From hence to Inverness
And bind us further to you.

MACBETH   The rest is labour which is not used for you;
I'll be myself the harbinger and make joyful   45
The hearing of my wife with your approach.
So humbly take my leave.

DUNCAN   My worthy Cawdor.

MACBETH   [*Aside*] The Prince of Cumberland: that is a step
On which I must fall down, or else o'erleap,
For in my way it lies. Stars, hide your fires,   50
Let not light see my black and deep desires,
The eye wink at the hand. Yet let that be,
Which the eye fears when it is done to see.   *Exit*

DUNCAN   True, worthy Banquo, he is full so valiant,
And in his commendations I am fed;   55
It is a banquet to me. Let's after him,
Whose care is gone before to bid us welcome:
It is a peerless kinsman.
                                        Flourish

                                                Exeunt

Lady Macbeth reads her husband's letter telling of the Witches' prophecy of kingship. She analyses his nature, fearing that he is too decent and squeamish to murder Duncan for the crown.

Characters

Lady Macbeth: first impressions (in pairs)

This is Lady Macbeth's first appearance. Some directors are keen to suggest that she is psychologically unstable right from the start, while others stress how close she is to her absent husband and how ambitious she is for both of them.

a Read lines 1–28, then write down your immediate thoughts on how Shakespeare presents this important character.

b With your partner, act out this speech. One person should perform the part of Lady Macbeth and the other should take the role of director.

c Write down your impressions of being both a director and an actor: what have you learned about Lady Macbeth?

Language in the play

Prose and verse (in pairs)

Macbeth's letter is in prose, but Lady Macbeth speaks in a much richer, poetic language. Look closely at the imagery she uses as she scrutinises her husband, almost as if he is present. With a partner, talk about Lady Macbeth's evaluation of his character. What does she see as his strengths? Perhaps more importantly, what does she consider his major failings? Draw up a list of Macbeth's strengths and weaknesses, then compare your list with your partner's.

◀ **Lines 1–12 may be just part of Macbeth's letter, concerning only the Witches. What other news might he have reported to his wife?**

in the day of success on the day of victory in battle
perfectest report most reliable source of information

missives messengers

the coming on of time the future

What thou art promised king

catch the nearest way act without pity
illness evil
holily fairly, without evil

Hie hurry

chastise punish and remove
golden round crown
metaphysical supernatural
withal as well

tidings news

Act 1 Scene 5
Macbeth's castle at Inverness

Enter LADY MACBETH *alone, with a letter*

LADY MACBETH   [*Reads*] 'They met me in the day of success, and
I have learned by the perfectest report they have more in
them than mortal knowledge. When I burned in desire to
question them further, they made themselves air, into which
they vanished. Whiles I stood rapt in the wonder of it, came   5
missives from the king who all-hailed me Thane of Cawdor, by
which title before these weïrd sisters saluted me and referred
me to the coming on of time, with "Hail, king that shalt be."
This have I thought good to deliver thee, my dearest partner of
greatness, that thou mightst not lose the dues of rejoicing by   10
being ignorant of what greatness is promised thee. Lay it to thy
heart and farewell.'
    Glamis thou art, and Cawdor, and shalt be
    What thou art promised; yet do I fear thy nature,
    It is too full o'th'milk of human kindness   15
    To catch the nearest way. Thou wouldst be great,
    Art not without ambition, but without
    The illness should attend it. What thou wouldst highly,
    That wouldst thou holily; wouldst not play false,
    And yet wouldst wrongly win. Thou'dst have, great Glamis,   20
    That which cries, 'Thus thou must do' if thou have it;
    And that which rather thou dost fear to do,
    Than wishest should be undone. Hie thee hither,
    That I may pour my spirits in thine ear
    And chastise with the valour of my tongue   25
    All that impedes thee from the golden round,
    Which fate and metaphysical aid doth seem
    To have thee crowned withal.

Enter [ATTENDANT]

                              What is your tidings?

ATTENDANT   The king comes here tonight.

Stagecraft

Addressing the audience

Lady Macbeth's speech can be divided into three sections (lines 38–45, 45–8 and 48–52), each beginning with the word 'Come'. Some people think that Shakespeare did this deliberately, so that the actor playing Lady Macbeth could say essentially the same thing to the three different sections of the audience (the right, the centre and the left).

Write down a summary of each part of the speech. As you write, ask yourself if Lady Macbeth says anything new in each of these sections, or if she simply expresses the same desire each time.

Language in the play

Lady Macbeth's soliloquy (in threes)

Lines 36–52 form a **soliloquy** until Macbeth arrives. The language is excited and its rhythm is varied. The pace changes throughout, which adds to the sense of compressed time and of hurrying fate. This is a powerful speech, full of verbs and metaphors ('fill me from the crown to the toe', 'make thick my blood', 'Shake', 'take my milk for gall'), and it reaches a climax with 'Hold, hold'.

In groups of three, experiment with the pacing of this speech, taking it in turns to speak the various sections and thinking about which words you would stress. Discuss your choices with the rest of the group.

1 Ambitious or evil? (in pairs)

a With a partner, discuss what you think Lady Macbeth most wants, and consider how this challenges conventional views of feminine behaviour. Remember that when the play was written and first performed, all the parts were played by male actors. Does this affect your interpretation of the character of Lady Macbeth?

b Many people find this speech shocking. Pick out the images that you feel contribute most to this impression and sketch the ones you think are the most powerful. Share these with a partner and put together a wall display of the strongest and most shocking images.

had the speed of overtook

tending attention, accommodation

unsex me remove from me all feminine feelings

compunctious compassionate
visitings of nature natural feelings or tendencies
fell deadly
gall bitter poison

pall wrap (as in a funeral pall or cloak)
dunnest darkest
keen sharp (also eager)

all-hail hereafter future kingship

in the instant now

LADY MACBETH   Thou'rt mad to say it.
          Is not thy master with him? Who, were't so,   30
          Would have informed for preparation.
ATTENDANT So please you, it is true: our thane is coming.
          One of my fellows had the speed of him;
          Who almost dead for breath, had scarcely more
          Than would make up his message.
LADY MACBETH   Give him tending,   35
          He brings great news.

                                        Exit [*Attendant*]
                              The raven himself is hoarse
          That croaks the fatal entrance of Duncan
          Under my battlements. Come, you spirits
          That tend on mortal thoughts, unsex me here
          And fill me from the crown to the toe topfull   40
          Of direst cruelty; make thick my blood,
          Stop up th'access and passage to remorse
          That no compunctious visitings of nature
          Shake my fell purpose nor keep peace between
          Th'effect and it. Come to my woman's breasts   45
          And take my milk for gall, you murd'ring ministers,
          Wherever in your sightless substances
          You wait on nature's mischief. Come, thick night,
          And pall thee in the dunnest smoke of hell,
          That my keen knife see not the wound it makes,   50
          Nor heaven peep through the blanket of the dark,
          To cry, 'Hold, hold.'

                              Enter MACBETH
                              Great Glamis, worthy Cawdor,
          Greater than both by the all-hail hereafter,
          Thy letters have transported me beyond
          This ignorant present, and I feel now   55
          The future in the instant.
MACBETH   My dearest love,
          Duncan comes here tonight.
LADY MACBETH   And when goes hence?
MACBETH   Tomorrow, as he purposes.

Language in the play
Double meanings (in pairs)

Lady Macbeth's lines 64–8 are filled with double meaning: 'provided for' = fed (or killed); 'business' = feasting (or murder); 'dispatch' = being welcoming (or killing). Discuss why Shakespeare uses such phrases. Do you think it is because:

- Lady Macbeth is subtly testing Macbeth to see how he will respond to the suggestion that they kill Duncan?
- Lady Macbeth is still unsure of doing such a deed and so has to disguise her words, even to herself?
- Shakespeare is adding to the tension of the play – in showing that they have not decided what to do, there is still some uncertainty about how the action will unfold?

Experiment with different ways of staging these lines. Think about what might be motivating Lady Macbeth to speak in this way and how Macbeth would respond.

Themes
Appearance and reality (in threes)

Act 1 Scene 6 continues to develop the theme of appearance and reality that emerged at the end of the previous scene. Both Duncan and Banquo speak favourably of Macbeth's castle. Look closely at the glossary and discuss the use of:

- dramatic irony (the pleasant and healthy positioning of the castle)
- extended metaphor (the ideas of flight, freedom and protection suggested by the 'temple-haunting martlet' that nests and breeds under its shelter).

1 Don't trust appearances!

Work out how to stage lines 1–10 of Scene 6 to bring out the dramatic irony of Duncan's and Banquo's praise of the benign appearance of Macbeth's castle. Remember – the audience has just heard Lady Macbeth planning Duncan's murder with the words 'look like th'innocent flower, / But be the serpent under't' (look friendly, but act treacherously).

beguile deceive

solely sovereign sway have the command of a king

look up clear appear innocent

To alter ... fear a guilty face (favour) reveals itself (or fear results in a guilty face)

Hautboys musical instruments similar to oboes

torches suggests that the scene takes place at night

seat position, location

martlet martin (a migratory bird); also, in Shakespeare's time, someone who was easily fooled

approve prove

mansionry the state of a dwelling

jutty part of a building that projects outwards

frieze a decorative band

coign of vantage convenient place

pendent hanging

procreant cradle a nest

LADY MACBETH   O never
    Shall sun that morrow see.
    Your face, my thane, is as a book where men   60
    May read strange matters. To beguile the time,
    Look like the time, bear welcome in your eye,
    Your hand, your tongue; look like th'innocent flower,
    But be the serpent under't. He that's coming
    Must be provided for, and you shall put   65
    This night's great business into my dispatch,
    Which shall to all our nights and days to come
    Give solely sovereign sway and masterdom.
MACBETH   We will speak further –
LADY MACBETH   Only look up clear;
    To alter favour ever is to fear.   70
    Leave all the rest to me.

Exeunt

Act 1 Scene 6
Outside Macbeth's castle

Hautboys, and torches. Enter King DUNCAN, MALCOLM,
DONALDBAIN, BANQUO, LENNOX, MACDUFF, ROSS, ANGUS,
and attendants

DUNCAN   This castle hath a pleasant seat; the air
    Nimbly and sweetly recommends itself
    Unto our gentle senses.
BANQUO   This guest of summer,
    The temple-haunting martlet, does approve
    By his loved mansionry that the heaven's breath   5
    Smells wooingly here. No jutty, frieze,
    Buttress, nor coign of vantage but this bird
    Hath made his pendent bed and procreant cradle;
    Where they most breed and haunt, I have observed
    The air is delicate.   10

Lady Macbeth welcomes Duncan with elaborately courteous language. She speaks of loyalty, obedience and gratefulness for past honours.

1 Duncan beware! (in fours)

The script opposite has many instances of dramatic irony relating to the way that pleasing appearances can hide a darker reality. In your groups, two students read aloud the duologue between Duncan and Lady Macbeth, while the other two listen carefully and call out 'Duncan beware!' whenever they believe he has misjudged his hostess, or when she is being insincere. Write short notes to the actors playing the parts of Lady Macbeth and Duncan to explain how they should behave with each other.

Themes

Duncan and Lady Macbeth (in pairs)

This is the first and last time that Lady Macbeth and Duncan are seen to talk to each other. The language is formal, as you would expect between a king and his subject and a hostess and her guest. Even so, Shakespeare uses words that continue to develop key themes already explored in the play. Look carefully at the exchange between Duncan and Lady Macbeth, then discuss the following:

- the imagery of pursuit and hunting
- the theme of duty
- the use of the word 'love'.

2 Duncan's last night (by yourself)

Imagine you are Duncan staying with the Macbeths. Write his journal entry or a letter to his wife the night he arrives at Glamis Castle. What does he think of Macbeth? Lady Macbeth? The castle? While doing this, keep in mind the dramatic irony of what you write: Duncan does not know what his hosts have planned for him, but you do. Alternatively, write a 'deleted scene' in which Duncan talks about events so far and his plans for the future. Write this as a soliloquy in modern prose, modern poetry, or imitating Shakespeare's language in the rest of this scene.

The love ... thank as love the love offered is sometimes a burden but is still received gratefully

God yield us God reward me

single weak
contend balance, weigh
loads fills
those of old past honours
late dignities recent honours
We rest your hermits we will pray for you constantly
coursed chased, hunted
purveyor officer riding ahead to prepare food
holp helped

in count in trust (or totally)
make their audit show their accounts (or give to you)
Still always

By your leave with your permission

28

Enter LADY [MACBETH]

DUNCAN   See, see, our honoured hostess. – The love
              That follows us sometime is our trouble,
              Which still we thank as love. Herein I teach you
              How you shall bid God yield us for your pains
              And thank us for your trouble.

LADY MACBETH   All our service,   15
              In every point twice done and then done double,
              Were poor and single business to contend
              Against those honours deep and broad wherewith
              Your majesty loads our house. For those of old,
              And the late dignities heaped up to them,   20
              We rest your hermits.

DUNCAN   Where's the Thane of Cawdor?
              We coursed him at the heels and had a purpose
              To be his purveyor, but he rides well,
              And his great love, sharp as his spur, hath holp him
              To his home before us. Fair and noble hostess,   25
              We are your guest tonight.

LADY MACBETH   Your servants ever
              Have theirs, themselves, and what is theirs in count
              To make their audit at your highness' pleasure,
              Still to return your own.

DUNCAN   Give me your hand;
              Conduct me to mine host: we love him highly   30
              And shall continue our graces towards him.
              By your leave, hostess.

                                      Exeunt

Macbeth struggles with his conscience: killing Duncan will result in vengeance; there are compelling reasons against the murder. Heaven itself will abhor the deed. Only ambition spurs him on.

1 To kill or not to kill? (in small groups)

Macbeth agonises over killing Duncan. Experiment with ways of speaking his soliloquy to bring out his uneasy feelings. In groups of three or four, read aloud one sentence each, making sure you either use emphasis or pause where appropriate. Afterwards, write down as many reasons as you can think of for why Duncan should not be killed.

2 'A deed without a name' (in pairs)

In Act 4 Scene 1, line 48, the Witches talk of 'A deed without a name'. In the script opposite, Macbeth, like Lady Macbeth (Act 1 Scene 5, lines 61–8), seems unable to speak directly of killing Duncan. Instead, he uses less brutal language (including euphemism): 'it', 'assassination', 'his surcease', 'this blow', 'these cases', 'ingredience', 'the deed', 'bear the knife', 'his taking-off', 'horrid deed', 'my intent'.

Read the soliloquy but replace these euphemisms with the words 'killing Duncan'. Talk together about the effect this has on the soliloquy. Think of some modern euphemisms that say the same thing (they can be formal or informal phrases).

Hautboys. Torches.
stage directions call for musicians and light-bearers

trammel up the consequence be without consequences ('trammel' = a net to catch a bird or a cloth to wrap and bind a corpse)

his surcease Duncan's death

the be-all and the end-all the final act (without further consequences)

jump the life to come risk heaven's punishment

inventor originator of the action

chalice cup, goblet

faculties powers as king

clear innocent

his taking-off Duncan's murder

cherubin angelic children

sightless couriers the wind (also blind or invisible messengers)

no spur ... th'other I have no motivation to kill Duncan other than my own ambition

Act 1 Scene 7
Macbeth's castle Near the Great Hall

*Hautboys. Torches. Enter a butler and many servants with dishes
and service over the stage. Then enter* MACBETH

MACBETH If it were done when 'tis done, then 'twere well
It were done quickly. If th'assassination
Could trammel up the consequence and catch
With his surcease, success, that but this blow
Might be the be-all and the end-all – here,   5
But here, upon this bank and shoal of time,
We'd jump the life to come. But in these cases,
We still have judgement here that we but teach
Bloody instructions, which being taught, return
To plague th'inventor. This even-handed justice   10
Commends th'ingredience of our poisoned chalice
To our own lips. He's here in double trust:
First, as I am his kinsman and his subject,
Strong both against the deed; then, as his host,
Who should against his murderer shut the door,   15
Not bear the knife myself. Besides, this Duncan
Hath borne his faculties so meek, hath been
So clear in his great office, that his virtues
Will plead like angels, trumpet-tongued against
The deep damnation of his taking-off.   20
And pity, like a naked newborn babe
Striding the blast, or heaven's cherubin horsed
Upon the sightless couriers of the air,
Shall blow the horrid deed in every eye,
That tears shall drown the wind. I have no spur   25
To prick the sides of my intent, but only
Vaulting ambition which o'erleaps itself
And falls on th'other –

Enter LADY [MACBETH]

How now? What news?

Macbeth says he has decided not to kill Duncan. Lady Macbeth accuses him of cowardice and lack of manliness. She would kill her own child rather than break such a promise.

1 A wife taunts her husband (in small groups)

One person reads the part of Macbeth; all the others play Lady Macbeth. Macbeth sits or stands in the centre; the Lady Macbeths walk or stand around him. Work through lines 28–82, with each Lady Macbeth reading only up to a punctuation mark before handing on to another person. Deliver your words to Macbeth in any way you think appropriate. Afterwards, discuss which sentence or phrase of Lady Macbeth's you think has the greatest effect on Macbeth in making him decide to carry out the murder.

Language in the play
Shocking imagery

In this scene, Shakespeare uses imagery that links newborn babies, pity and violence. Look closely at lines 18–25 and lines 54–9 in this scene. Using a clean copy of these lines, underline the words that relate to this imagery and make notes in the margins. When you have done so, carry out the following activities.

a This is highly visceral language, but what is actually being said in these lines? Paraphrase the section so that you have a clear understanding of its meaning.

b What visual images do the lines evoke for you and why are these images shocking or strange? Discuss this in pairs.

c Write a paragraph exploring how Shakespeare's language creates vivid images that evoke complex responses in an audience and influence how we view the characters.

2 Did the Macbeths have children?

Imagery associated with children occurs throughout the play. Some critics have argued that the Macbeths are motivated by the loss of a child, but Shakespeare makes very little of this.

Do you think it helps us understand their behaviour if we believe they have lost a child, or is it unimportant? Write an imagined secret history of the Macbeths – their untold story – in a few paragraphs.

I have bought … so soon I want to enjoy my improved reputation, not throw it away so quickly

green and pale sickly

afeard afraid

valour worth or importance due to personal qualities or rank

the ornament of life life's highest achievement (the crown)

the poor cat i'th'adage the adage referred to is a proverb about a cat who wanted to fish but was afraid of water

break this enterprise suggest killing Duncan

Did then adhere were at that time convenient

They have made themselves now the time and place (to murder Duncan) present themselves

fitness timeliness

given suck breastfed

had I so sworn if I had promised

LADY MACBETH   He has almost supped. Why have you left the chamber?

MACBETH   Hath he asked for me?

LADY MACBETH   Know you not, he has?   30

MACBETH   We will proceed no further in this business.
He hath honoured me of late, and I have bought
Golden opinions from all sorts of people,
Which would be worn now in their newest gloss,
Not cast aside so soon.

LADY MACBETH   Was the hope drunk   35
Wherein you dressed yourself? Hath it slept since?
And wakes it now to look so green and pale
At what it did so freely? From this time,
Such I account thy love. Art thou afeard
To be the same in thine own act and valour,   40
As thou art in desire? Wouldst thou have that
Which thou esteem'st the ornament of life,
And live a coward in thine own esteem,
Letting I dare not wait upon I would,
Like the poor cat i'th'adage?

MACBETH   Prithee, peace.   45
I dare do all that may become a man;
Who dares do more is none.

LADY MACBETH   What beast was't then
That made you break this enterprise to me?
When you durst do it, then you were a man.
And to be more than what you were, you would   50
Be so much more the man. Nor time, nor place
Did then adhere, and yet you would make both.
They have made themselves and that their fitness now
Does unmake you. I have given suck and know
How tender 'tis to love the babe that milks me: 55
I would, while it was smiling in my face,
Have plucked my nipple from his boneless gums
And dashed the brains out, had I so sworn
As you have done to this.

Lady Macbeth will make the king's bodyguards so drunk that murdering Duncan (and blaming the bodyguards) will be easy. Macbeth applauds her. He says that they should veil their evil designs with pleasant looks.

1 'We fail?' (in small groups)

There are many ways of speaking these two words. Explore them using your own approaches. You might want to say them as a simple statement of resignation, as a question or with scorn.

2 The art of questioning (in pairs)

Macbeth and Lady Macbeth use questions for different purposes in this scene. As you read through the script opposite, consider different ways of delivering each of these questions. Experiment with Macbeth having trouble maintaining eye contact, or with Lady Macbeth moving around freely while Macbeth stands still, or with both characters staring intently at each other throughout the duologue. What do you think is the state of mind of each character in this section? What is their motivation?

Write about it

'Bring forth men-children only' (in pairs)

Lady Macbeth convinces her husband to murder Duncan. Macbeth, in turn, praises her strength of character. Write one paragraph each answering the following questions:

- What do Macbeth's words in lines 72–4 tell us about the position of women in Scotland at the time the play is set? Refer to Lady Macbeth's speech in Act 1 Scene 5, lines 36–52 to support your points.
- What does this section tell us about the relationship between Lady Macbeth and her husband?

3 Imagery

Lady Macbeth uses two metaphors familiar to Jacobean audiences:

- 'But screw your courage to the sticking-place' (line 60) suggests an archer turning the screw of his crossbow to adjust the cord to receive an arrow, or a musician tightening the strings of a violin.
- Lines 65–7 use an elaborate image from alchemy. Drunkenness will make the king's attendants forget their duties because noxious vapours will befuddle their reason ('memory, the warder of the brain, / Shall be a fume'). 'Receipt' and 'limbeck' were items of apparatus used by alchemists.

As you read through the rest of the play, look out for other examples of imagery that you think might have struck a particular chord with audiences in Shakespeare's day.

But only

screw … sticking-place fix your courage firmly in place so it can't move

chamberlains attendants, bodyguards

wassail drinking

convince overpower

warder guard or keeper

fume it was believed that the fumes from alcohol caused drunkenness

receipt receptacle

limbeck a device used in distilling alcohol

swinish sleep sleeping (and snoring) like pigs

drenchèd drunken

put upon impose

spongy drink-sodden

quell slaughter, murder

mettle spirit

received interpreted

clamour loud shouting or outcry

settled unchanging

bend up get ready (to make tense like the frame of a bow)

Each corporal agent every part of me

mock the time deceive the world

MACBETH   If we should fail?

LADY MACBETH   We fail?

But screw your courage to the sticking-place,   60
And we'll not fail. When Duncan is asleep,
Whereto the rather shall his day's hard journey
Soundly invite him, his two chamberlains
Will I with wine and wassail so convince
That memory, the warder of the brain,   65
Shall be a fume, and the receipt of reason
A limbeck only. When in swinish sleep
Their drenchèd natures lies as in a death,
What cannot you and I perform upon
Th'unguarded Duncan? What not put upon   70
His spongy officers, who shall bear the guilt
Of our great quell?

MACBETH   Bring forth men-children only,
For thy undaunted mettle should compose
Nothing but males. Will it not be received,
When we have marked with blood those sleepy two   75
Of his own chamber, and used their very daggers,
That they have done't?

LADY MACBETH   Who dares receive it other,
As we shall make our griefs and clamour roar
Upon his death?

MACBETH   I am settled and bend up
Each corporal agent to this terrible feat.   80
Away, and mock the time with fairest show,
False face must hide what the false heart doth know.

Exeunt

Looking back at Act 1
Activities for groups or individuals

1 Contrasting scenes

Shakespeare uses the dramatic technique of juxtaposing scenes: each scene contrasts with, or comments on, the preceding scene. For example, the ghostly supernatural world of Scene 1 is followed by the harsh military world of Scene 2 (the former is entirely made up of female characters, the latter of male characters). Write a tabloid newspaper headline for each scene in Act 1. For example, Scene 2 could be: '*Victory! Captain tells of amazing win for Duncan's men.*'

2 Witches: stereotypes and conventions

Although the Witches have many stereotypical features of historical witches (see p. 8), they are only called 'witch' once in the play (Scene 3, line 5). Later on they call themselves the 'weïrd sisters' (Scene 3, line 30) and are called 'weïrd women' by Banquo (Act 3 Scene 1, line 2), which in Anglo-Saxon mythology referred to the goddess Fate, or 'Wyrd'.

Look at the images of the Witches in different productions on the page opposite and in the photo gallery at the beginning of this book. Write a paragraph explaining how you would portray them. Select descriptions of the Witches from the play to support your decisions.

3 Imagery

In Act 1, imagery that links pity, milk, blood and babies provokes strong responses from us. Find examples of this imagery, then carry out the activities below.

a Create a tableau based on one example. Try to capture the symbolism rather than an exact representation. Be as imaginative as you can.

b Pick out phrases or sentences that strike you and explain why they have this effect. Is it the visual image they conjure up, the way the words sound, the repetition or the vocabulary?

4 Men and women

In Macbeth's world, what qualities does a 'man' have? What qualities does a 'woman' have? Copy the table below and add examples. Some have been provided for you.

	What qualities?	Who has them?	Where are they?
Man	Bravery	Macbeth	1.2.16
	Ruthlessness	Lady Macbeth	2.2.55–60
Woman	Manipulative	Lady Macbeth	1.5.60–8
	Deceitful	Lady Macbeth	1.6.15–21

Discuss how Macbeth and Lady Macbeth conform to these ideas at the beginning and end of Act 1. Have they changed over the course of this act? Has Shakespeare challenged traditional ideas of 'masculinity' and 'femininity'?

5 Act 1 on screen

a Watch the openings of two different movie adaptations of *Macbeth*, then discuss which is the most effective and why. You may want to consider:

- the craft of filmmaking: the setting, soundtrack, camera angles and lighting
- any changes made to Shakespeare's script.

b Imagine you are a director working on a new film of *Macbeth*. Which actors would you choose to play Macbeth and Lady Macbeth? Who would you cast as Duncan and Banquo? Why? You may also want to think about *when* and *where* you would set it: for example, would you set your version in medieval Scotland or modern-day America? Now discuss these choices in groups.

Language in the play

'husbandry in heaven' (in pairs)

The opening duologue between Banquo and his son, Fleance, describes the threatening atmosphere. Darkness has been associated with evil before (in Act 1 Scene 4, lines 50–1 and Scene 5, line 48), but here it seems even more ominous. In pairs, analyse the language that Banquo and Fleance use to describe the intensity of the night. What themes are explored through this imagery? How effectively does it create the mood of this scene?

Characters

Banquo and Macbeth (in threes)

Here, Shakespeare dramatises the difference between Banquo, the honourable man and protective father, and Macbeth, the deceiver (who is alone). Banquo uses kind and open words in his report of Duncan ('He hath been in unusual pleasure'); he wishes to stay free of guilt ('keep / My bosom franchised') and remain loyal ('allegiance clear') to Duncan. Tellingly, he asks for his sword when Macbeth appears. In sharp contrast, Macbeth speaks untruths: 'A friend'; 'Being unprepared'; 'I think not of them'. He tries to tempt Banquo to his side ('cleave to my consent') in return for honour (lines 25–6).

Write advice for the actors on how to show the men's increasingly uneasy relationship, and how to alert the audience to the contrast between them. How would you position the actors? Would they speak face to face throughout these lines? How would you convey their real intentions? In groups of three (with Banquo, Macbeth and the director) create tableaux, taking it in turns to swap roles to try out different interpretations.

1 Fleance's point of view (in pairs)

Discuss how much you think Fleance knows: what does he make of the conversation between his father and Macbeth? Then write a diary entry of at least 100 words, in which Fleance describes what he sees, hears and feels about lines 10–30.

she the moon

husbandry thriftiness (in putting out the light of the stars)

A heavy summons … sleep despite being weighed down with a heavy tiredness, I cannot sleep

merciful … repose I call upon the angels of heaven to banish the dark thoughts I have increasingly had

largess to your offices generous gifts to the servants who have waited on you

withal as well, too

shut up gone to bed

Being unprepared … wrought because Duncan's visit was unexpected, we were unable to entertain him as fully as we would have wished

So I lose none … counselled as long as I remain loyal to the king, I will be able to talk about 'honour' with you

franchised free from obligation

Act 2 Scene 1
Macbeth's castle The courtyard

Enter BANQUO, *and* FLEANCE *with a torch-bearer before him*

BANQUO	How goes the night, boy?
FLEANCE	The moon is down; I have not heard the clock.
BANQUO	And she goes down at twelve.
FLEANCE	I take't, 'tis later, sir.
BANQUO	Hold, take my sword. – There's husbandry in heaven,

Their candles are all out. – Take thee that too.   5
A heavy summons lies like lead upon me,
And yet I would not sleep; merciful powers,
Restrain in me the cursèd thoughts that nature
Gives way to in repose.

Enter MACBETH, *and a Servant with a torch*

                Give me my sword –
Who's there?   10

MACBETH	A friend.
BANQUO	What, sir, not yet at rest? The king's abed.

He hath been in unusual pleasure
And sent forth great largess to your offices.
This diamond he greets your wife withal,   15
      [*Gives Macbeth a diamond*]
By the name of most kind hostess, and shut up
In measureless content.

MACBETH	Being unprepared,

Our will became the servant to defect,
Which else should free have wrought.

BANQUO	All's well.

I dreamed last night of the three weïrd sisters;   20
To you they have showed some truth.

MACBETH	I think not of them;

Yet when we can entreat an hour to serve,
We would spend it in some words upon that business,
If you would grant the time.

BANQUO	At your kind'st leisure.
MACBETH	If you shall cleave to my consent, when 'tis, 25

It shall make honour for you.

BANQUO	So I lose none

In seeking to augment it, but still keep
My bosom franchised and allegiance clear,
I shall be counselled.

Alone, Macbeth hallucinates, thinking he sees a blood-stained dagger. As he moves to murder Duncan, his thoughts are filled with evil images.

1 Macbeth sees the dagger (in pairs)

Macbeth's hallucination of the dagger is both a warning and an invitation. At first he dismisses the 'fatal vision' as something created by his unreliable senses, but soon he becomes convinced that he has to murder Duncan.

With a partner, discuss the various turning points in this soliloquy. Consider the issues Macbeth raises and how he answers them, then write these down in a list with two columns (issues and answers). Compare the points you have listed with those identified by others in your class.

2 Acting the horror (in small groups, then by yourself)

Work out your own presentation of Macbeth's soliloquy. Use the following ideas to help you:

- As one person reads the soliloquy a short section at a time, others silently act out what Macbeth does at each moment.
- Allocate short sections of the soliloquy to different members of the group. Each person should deliver their lines in a different style (for example, lines 33–4 could be spoken in horror, or in fear, or with faltering control). Experiment with the volume, pitch and pace of this speech in your performance.

After the presentations, write a detailed account of the one you found most interesting or dramatic. Why were some presentations more successful than others?

Stagecraft

Is there a dagger on the stage? (by yourself)

Think about how you would stage lines 33–47 to greatest dramatic effect. Should a dagger actually be shown on stage (for example, as a holograph)? What sound effects might you add at particular lines? Write a letter to a director describing your views about the use of props, sound effects, lighting and Macbeth's movement on the stage in the script opposite.

fatal vision deadly sight

sensible / To feeling able to be touched

heat-oppressèd feverish

yet still

palpable real, physical, touchable

dudgeon handle

gouts large drops

one half-world night-time world

Hecate goddess of witchcraft

off'rings gifts, sacrifices

Alarumed alerted, awoken

sentinel guard

Tarquin a Roman prince who raped Lucrece

prate talk

knell funeral bell

MACBETH   Good repose the while.

BANQUO   Thanks, sir; the like to you. 30

[Exeunt] Banquo[, Fleance, and Torch-bearer]

MACBETH   *[To Servant]* Go bid thy mistress, when my drink is ready,
She strike upon the bell. Get thee to bed.

Exit [Servant]

Is this a dagger which I see before me,
The handle toward my hand? Come, let me clutch thee:
I have thee not, and yet I see thee still. 35
Art thou not, fatal vision, sensible
To feeling as to sight? Or art thou but
A dagger of the mind, a false creation,
Proceeding from the heat-oppressèd brain?
I see thee yet, in form as palpable 40
As this which now I draw.
Thou marshall'st me the way that I was going,
And such an instrument I was to use.
Mine eyes are made the fools o'th'other senses,
Or else worth all the rest. I see thee still, 45
And on thy blade and dudgeon gouts of blood,
Which was not so before. There's no such thing:
It is the bloody business which informs
Thus to mine eyes. Now o'er the one half-world
Nature seems dead, and wicked dreams abuse 50
The curtained sleep. Witchcraft celebrates
Pale Hecate's off'rings, and withered murder,
Alarumed by his sentinel, the wolf,
Whose howl's his watch, thus with his stealthy pace,
With Tarquin's ravishing strides, towards his design 55
Moves like a ghost. Thou sure and firm-set earth,
Hear not my steps, which way they walk, for fear
Thy very stones prate of my whereabout,
And take the present horror from the time,
Which now suits with it. Whiles I threat, he lives; 60
Words to the heat of deeds too cold breath gives.

A bell rings

I go, and it is done. The bell invites me.
Hear it not, Duncan, for it is a knell
That summons thee to heaven or to hell.   *Exit*

Lady Macbeth, exhilarated by drink, awaits Macbeth's return from Duncan's room. She has drugged Duncan's bodyguards, but fears that the murder has not been done. Macbeth returns and says he has killed the king.

1 Offstage murder (in pairs)

Once again a major event – Duncan's murder – takes place off stage. Why do you think Shakespeare does this? Is it to preserve the dignity of Duncan (and of monarchy)? Is it to shield us from the true horror of Macbeth's crime? Talk about this with a partner, and then compile a list of the elements of stagecraft that make this scene so dramatically effective.

Write about it
Language and meaning

Analyse the language used by Macbeth and Lady Macbeth. Write two paragraphs on each character, detailing what you have learned about them by line 24. Below are some points you might want to consider:

- Even though she has been drinking, Lady Macbeth's opening two lines appear carefully composed. Look not only at their meaning but also at their structure. Contrast them with Macbeth's lines.
- Why does Lady Macbeth decide not to kill Duncan herself? What does this tell us about her? Compare her words here with her speeches in Act 1 Scene 7.

Stagecraft
After the murder (in pairs)

Take parts as Lady Macbeth and Macbeth. Read straight through the whole of Scene 2. (Don't pause to worry over words you are not sure of.) What should be the pace of playing different sections of the scene? Write notes advising the actors where and why they might speak quickly, and where they could adopt a different style of speech.

2 Stichomythia (in pairs)

Lines 13–24 alternate rapidly between Macbeth and Lady Macbeth to increase pace and tension. They are an example of **stichomythia** and are usually spoken quickly on stage. As you read these lines aloud, make a list of words that describe how you feel and how an audience might feel on hearing these lines. Then draft your own dialogue between two frightened or two guilty people who find themselves in a dark and dangerous situation.

quenched silenced, drugged

fatal bellman watchman who rang a bell the night before a prisoner was executed

stern'st good-night death, the last goodnight of all

surfeited filled up, overindulged

grooms Duncan's bodyguards

mock their charge abandon their duties

possets hot drinks of milk with wine, sugar and spices

Alack … done I am sure the guards have woken up and we have failed

Confounds us overthrows, ruins us

owl, crickets (creatures often associated with death)

sorry miserable, painful

42

Act 2 Scene 2
Macbeth's castle Near Duncan's room

Enter LADY MACBETH

LADY MACBETH That which hath made them drunk, hath made me
        bold;
    What hath quenched them, hath given me fire.
        [*An owl shrieks*]
                                    Hark, peace!
    It was the owl that shrieked, the fatal bellman
    Which gives the stern'st good-night. He is about it.
    The doors are open, and the surfeited grooms 5
    Do mock their charge with snores. I have drugged their
        possets,
    That death and nature do contend about them,
    Whether they live, or die.

Enter MACBETH [*with two bloody daggers*]

MACBETH   Who's there? What ho?

LADY MACBETH Alack, I am afraid they have awaked,
    And 'tis not done; th'attempt and not the deed 10
    Confounds us. Hark! I laid their daggers ready,
    He could not miss 'em. Had he not resembled
    My father as he slept, I had done't. My husband?

MACBETH I have done the deed. Didst thou not hear a noise?

LADY MACBETH I heard the owl scream and the crickets cry. 15
    Did not you speak?

MACBETH When?

LADY MACBETH Now.

MACBETH As I descended?

LADY MACBETH Ay. 20

MACBETH Hark, who lies i'th'second chamber?

LADY MACBETH Donaldbain.

MACBETH This is a sorry sight.

LADY MACBETH A foolish thought, to say a sorry sight.

Characters

Does Macbeth have a conscience? (in pairs)

Macbeth seems suddenly conscience-stricken: he is unable to say 'Amen', and cannot pray. Not being able to say 'Amen' suggests that God has already judged him and condemned him to eternal damnation. Many actors portray Macbeth talking to himself, ignoring his wife. Others show him almost obsessively telling her his story.

a   Discuss how you would act lines 25–46 to show how each character is developing and how their relationship has suddenly changed due to their murderous act.

b   Read through Macbeth's lines, with one person in role as Macbeth and the other person speaking the words of his conscience at the end of each line, asking questions to reveal what he is really feeling.

1 Images of sleep (in groups of four or more)

In lines 38–43, Shakespeare uses vivid images to portray sleep.

a   Sleep deprivation is used as a form of torture. Discuss with others in your group what you think are the psychological effects of loss of sleep; you could research this outside the classroom.

b   How do you visualise these images? Try drawing them very quickly and showing them to the rest of the group. How do they compare with Shakespeare's words? What is lost and what is gained by turning them into pictures?

c   Work out a mime for each image. Extend your mime by adding the results of lack of sleep promised by the First Witch in Act 1 Scene 3, lines 18–22.

◄ 'Why did you bring these daggers?' What postures do you think the Macbeths should have at this point in the play?

addressed them prepared themselves

hangman's hands blood-covered hands (executioners often disembowelled condemned men)

Methought I thought

ravelled sleeve frayed sleeve, or tangled silk

death of each day's life sleep is to the day what death is to life

sore labour's bath hard work's cure

Balm healing medicine

second course main part of a meal

unbend relax, weaken

filthy witness evidence (blood)

MACBETH   There's one did laugh in's sleep, and one cried, 'Murder!',   25
               That they did wake each other; I stood, and heard them,
               But they did say their prayers and addressed them
               Again to sleep.

LADY MACBETH   There are two lodged together.

MACBETH   One cried 'God bless us!' and 'Amen' the other,
               As they had seen me with these hangman's hands.   30
               List'ning their fear, I could not say 'Amen'
               When they did say 'God bless us.'

LADY MACBETH   Consider it not so deeply.

MACBETH   But wherefore could not I pronounce 'Amen'?
               I had most need of blessing and 'Amen'   35
               Stuck in my throat.

LADY MACBETH   These deeds must not be thought
               After these ways; so, it will make us mad.

MACBETH   Methought I heard a voice cry, 'Sleep no more:
               Macbeth does murder sleep', the innocent sleep,
               Sleep that knits up the ravelled sleeve of care,   40
               The death of each day's life, sore labour's bath,
               Balm of hurt minds, great nature's second course,
               Chief nourisher in life's feast.

LADY MACBETH   What do you mean?

MACBETH   Still it cried, 'Sleep no more' to all the house;
               'Glamis hath murdered sleep', and therefore Cawdor   45
               Shall sleep no more: Macbeth shall sleep no more.

LADY MACBETH   Who was it, that thus cried? Why, worthy thane,
               You do unbend your noble strength to think
               So brain-sickly of things. Go get some water
               And wash this filthy witness from your hand.   50
               Why did you bring these daggers from the place?
               They must lie there. Go carry them and smear
               The sleepy grooms with blood.

MACBETH   I'll go no more.
               I am afraid to think what I have done;
               Look on't again, I dare not.

Themes

Masculinity and femininity (in groups of five or six)

This is an important scene for many reasons, but in particular for how we view the two central characters. We might expect Lady Macbeth to be more shaken than her husband, the warrior, by Duncan's murder, but the opposite seems to be true. Look at lines 47–53, 55–60 and 67–75, then discuss how and why Shakespeare seems to challenge traditional views of masculine and feminine behaviour.

- Does Lady Macbeth understand the full implications of Macbeth's actions?
- Has Lady Macbeth's wish to be 'unsexed' in Act 1 Scene 5, line 39 come true?
- Is she behaving in this way to protect her husband as well as herself?
- Are her actions those of a rational individual?

Now create your own list of questions to ask the Macbeths at this point in the play. You should aim to explore the characters' motivations, inner logic and unexpressed feelings. Take turns to step into role as either Lady Macbeth or Macbeth and sit in the hot-seat, ready to answer questions from the rest of your group.

1 Guilty – and guiltier? (whole class)

Divide into two groups to stage a debate. One group argues that Lady Macbeth is morally less defensible than her husband by the end of this scene. The other half of the class takes the opposite view: that Macbeth is the guiltier of the two. If you use quotations from the script to support your argument, make them no more than five words long. Write notes about which arguments you find the most convincing. At the end of the debate take a vote to find out which character the class feels is most guilty.

Language in the play

Images of death

Look closely at the language used by both Lady Macbeth and Macbeth, focusing in particular on lines 56–8 and 63–6. Write two paragraphs analysing the imagery used by both characters. Which character do you think best understands the reality of the situation? Or are they both delusional? Explain your reasons with evidence from the script.

Infirm hesitating, wavering

'tis the eye … devil it is childish to fear something that looks horrible but cannot harm you

gild paint (in this case with blood – possibly a pun on gild/guilt)

withal with it (blood)

appals terrifies

Neptune god of the sea

multitudinous seas the many oceans of the earth

incarnadine redden

Making the green one red staining the green sea red with blood

I shame I would be ashamed

Your constancy … unattended you have lost your nerve

lest occasion call us in case the discovery of the murder causes us to be sent for

to be watchers to be awake

To know my deed … self if I accept my crime, I have to accept my new identity as a murderer

LADY MACBETH   Infirm of purpose!   55
Give me the daggers. The sleeping and the dead
Are but as pictures; 'tis the eye of childhood
That fears a painted devil. If he do bleed,
I'll gild the faces of the grooms withal,
For it must seem their guilt.   *Exit*
                          Knock within
MACBETH   Whence is that knocking?   60
How is't with me, when every noise appals me?
What hands are here? Ha: they pluck out mine eyes.
Will all great Neptune's ocean wash this blood
Clean from my hand? No: this my hand will rather
The multitudinous seas incarnadine,   65
Making the green one red.

                    Enter LADY [MACBETH]

LADY MACBETH   My hands are of your colour, but I shame
To wear a heart so white.
                    Knock [*within*]
                              I hear a knocking
At the south entry. Retire we to our chamber;
A little water clears us of this deed.   70
How easy is it then! Your constancy
Hath left you unattended.
                    Knock [*within*]
                              Hark, more knocking.
Get on your night-gown, lest occasion call us
And show us to be watchers. Be not lost
So poorly in your thoughts.   75
MACBETH   To know my deed, 'twere best not know my self.
                    Knock [*within*]
Wake Duncan with thy knocking: I would thou couldst.
                                        Exeunt

Stagecraft

The Porter: comic relief? (in small groups)

Some directors cut the 'Porter scene' because they consider it irrelevant to the action. Read the scene, then discuss why you think Shakespeare wrote it. Here are some ideas to help you:

- **Light relief** Given the intensity of the play, this comes as a welcome moment of humour. Also, Shakespeare's theatre company – the King's Men – always had one actor who specialised in comic parts. Here, the Porter acts as the funny man to Macduff's straight man.
- **Dramatic function** The Porter's scene further develops key themes in the play, including damnation ('th'everlasting bonfire'), the supernatural ('Beelzebub'), ambition (the greedy farmer), deceit (the equivocator), theft (the tailor), desire and achievement (lust and the effects that drink has on it). The Porter's use of bathos (the sudden descent from the sublime to the absurd) slows the action and, in doing so, heightens the tension as we wait to see what happens next.
- **A link with older plays** In medieval mystery plays, a porter admitted sinners to hell. Here, Shakespeare links Macbeth's castle with hell. (See 'The Contexts of *Macbeth*', pp. 164–5.)

1 Acting it out (in pairs or small groups)

Break down the language in the Porter's speech to make it as vivid as possible. You could have two or more people miming the actions described, or have just one person responding as someone else reads the words aloud. Use your imagination, and make it as funny as you can!

Language in the play

Verse and prose

The Porter's colloquial vocabulary and imagery are a sharp contrast to the dense, poetic imagery of the previous scene. His rambling prose is further contrasted with the sharp, repetitive beat of the banging at the gate. Rewrite one or two extracts from Macbeth's soliloquy in Scene 1, lines 33–61 to show how it may have sounded in prose (in the way the Porter speaks). What have you discovered about the distinction between Shakespeare's poetry and prose?

old plenty of

Beelzebub the Devil

th'expectation of plenty the expectation of a good harvest (which would have brought down the farmer's prices)

Faith a mild swear word, but it also contrasts with hell

equivocator liar; this seems to be a reference to Henry Garnet, a priest who tried to lie his way out of being involved in the Gunpowder Plot but was hanged in 1606

scales weighing scales, scales of justice

French hose baggy trousers

primrose way easy road

everlasting bonfire eternal damnation in hell

carousing drinking

second cock 3 a.m.

Marry by the Virgin Mary

nose-painting the reddening of the nose through an excess of drink

Lechery lust

mars stops

takes him off makes him sexually impotent

Act 2 Scene 3
The entrance to Macbeth's castle

Enter a PORTER. *Knocking within*

PORTER   Here's a knocking indeed: if a man were porter of hell-gate, he should have old turning the key. (*Knock*) Knock, knock, knock. Who's there i'th'name of Beelzebub? Here's a farmer that hanged himself on th'expectation of plenty. Come in time – have napkins enough about you, here you'll sweat for't. (*Knock*) Knock, knock. Who's there in th'other devil's name? Faith, here's an equivocator that could swear in both the scales against either scale, who committed treason enough for God's sake, yet could not equivocate to heaven. O, come in, equivocator. (*Knock*) Knock, knock, knock. Who's there? Faith, here's an English tailor come hither for stealing out of a French hose. Come in, tailor, here you may roast your goose. (*Knock*) Knock, knock. Never at quiet: what are you? But this place is too cold for hell. I'll devil-porter it no further: I had thought to have let in some of all professions that go the primrose way to th'everlasting bonfire. (*Knock*) Anon, anon. I pray you, remember the porter. [*Opens door*]   5   10   15

Enter MACDUFF *and* LENNOX

MACDUFF   Was it so late, friend, ere you went to bed,
That you do lie so late?

PORTER   Faith, sir, we were carousing till the second cock, and drink, sir, is a great provoker of three things.   20

MACDUFF   What three things does drink especially provoke?

PORTER   Marry, sir, nose-painting, sleep, and urine. Lechery, sir, it provokes, and unprovokes: it provokes the desire, but it takes away the performance. Therefore much drink may be said to be an equivocator with lechery: it makes him, and it mars him; it sets him on, and it takes him off; it persuades him and disheartens him, makes him stand to and not stand to. In conclusion, equivocates him in a sleep, and giving him the lie, leaves him.   25   30

Macduff has come to meet Duncan. Macbeth shows him to Duncan's room. Lennox tells of the terrible events of the night. Horrified, Macduff returns from Duncan's room.

1 'the earth / Was feverous and did shake'
(in small groups)

Lines 46–53 describe the terrible night that Lennox has experienced. In small groups, carry out *one* of the following activities.

a As one person speaks Lennox's lines, the others provide appropriate sound effects.

b Create a picture that conveys the horror of the night. Select images from the script that develop the dark mood. Either draw the images or create a collage with pictures from the Internet or magazines.

2 Another transition (in threes)

This part of the scene acts as an important transition: the Porter's humorous interlude breaks the tension between the murder scene and the scene in which the murder is discovered. In groups of three, act out lines 35–55. Think carefully about how Macbeth would behave in light of what he has just done. There is strong emphasis on dramatic irony here, but to what extent do you think Macbeth should behave differently?

◀ The Porter is usually portrayed as a comic figure, but some productions choose to depict him in a more sober way. How would the Porter in your own production behave?

Write about it

The divine right of kings (by yourself)

Find out more about the divine right of kings in Shakespeare's time, focusing on the possible consequences to a nation if that right is challenged (as Macbeth has done). Now think about why Shakespeare may have wanted to link the murderous events that have just taken place with the wider world. What would be the effect on Shakespeare's audience (including the king and courtiers)? Write two short paragraphs exploring possible links between the killing of Duncan and the 'dire combustion and confused events' that Lennox describes.

gave thee the lie knocked you out

requited him for his lie paid him back for his wrestling trick

took up my legs made me unable to stand

cast throw down, or throw up (be sick, vomit)

timely early

The labour ... pain the work I enjoy cures pain

limited appointed

dire combustion terrible fires and explosions (possibly an echo of the Gunpowder Plot)

obscure bird owl (associated with death)

livelong long-lasting

feverous feverish, diseased

'Twas a rough night Macbeth's statement is flat and laconic

Tongue ... thee this is beyond articulation and understanding

MACDUFF	I believe drink gave thee the lie last night.
PORTER	That it did, sir, i'the very throat on me, but I requited him for his lie, and, I think, being too strong for him, though he took up my legs sometime, yet I made a shift to cast him.

Enter MACBETH

MACDUFF	Is thy master stirring?	35
	Our knocking has awaked him: here he comes.	

[*Exit Porter*]

LENNOX	Good morrow, noble sir.
MACBETH	Good morrow, both.
MACDUFF	Is the king stirring, worthy thane?
MACBETH	Not yet.
MACDUFF	He did command me to call timely on him;
	I have almost slipped the hour.

MACBETH	I'll bring you to him. 40
MACDUFF	I know this is a joyful trouble to you, but yet 'tis one.
MACBETH	The labour we delight in physics pain. This is the door.
MACDUFF	I'll make so bold to call, for 'tis my limited service. *Exit*
LENNOX	Goes the king hence today?
MACBETH	He does – he did appoint so. 45
LENNOX	The night has been unruly: where we lay,
	Our chimneys were blown down, and, as they say,
	Lamentings heard i'th'air, strange screams of death
	And prophesying with accents terrible
	Of dire combustion and confused events, 50
	New hatched to th'woeful time. The obscure bird
	Clamoured the livelong night. Some say, the earth
	Was feverous and did shake.
MACBETH	'Twas a rough night.
LENNOX	My young remembrance cannot parallel
	A fellow to it. 55

Enter MACDUFF

MACDUFF	O horror, horror, horror,
	Tongue nor heart cannot conceive, nor name thee.
MACBETH *and* LENNOX	What's the matter?

1 'Confusion now hath made his masterpiece'

Macduff imagines 'Confusion' as a perverse artist who has created a 'masterpiece'. To gain a sense of the great confusion that results from Duncan's murder, try the following activity. You will need a large space such as a hall or drama studio (a cleared classroom will also be fine).

Everybody reads the whole page opposite, but each person begins at a different line. Start anywhere you wish in lines 59–83. As you walk around the room, greet others with a single line or sentence from the script. They will reply with a different line or sentence. Then move on to greet others. Greet as many people as you can, using a different line from the script each time. Keep the activity going for several minutes, then meet in small groups of four or five. Read through again, taking turns to read a sentence at a time. After your activity:

• Identify as many images as you can, and suggest what each describes.
• Write notes on how to stage the lines for greatest dramatic effect.

Language in the play

'Murder and treason!' (in pairs)

Macduff's language in lines 67–74 is dramatic and urgent. As well as waking the sleepers of the house, he compares the horror of 'death itself' with popular images of death and Judgement Day.

a Identify the language features in this section that suggest chaos, urgency and clamour.

b Look at the 'great doom's image' as depicted on the wall of the Guild Chapel in Stratford-upon-Avon, next door to Shakespeare's school (p. 164). Identify the details that are referenced in the script opposite.

Characters

'gentle lady'? (by yourself)

Macduff calls Lady Macbeth 'gentle' and says the news is too cruel for a woman's hearing (lines 76–9). From your knowledge of her so far, write some notes to the actor playing Lady Macbeth. How would you advise her to behave in this part of the scene? Write down between five and ten adjectives other than 'gentle' that you think appropriately describe her at this point in the play.

Confusion chaos

sacrilegious unholy

ope open

The Lord's anointed temple Duncan's body (the king was seen as God's anointed representative on Earth)

Gorgon (from Greek mythology) Medusa, a female monster with snakes instead of hair, who turned anyone who saw her into stone; the same will happen to anyone who sees Duncan

Shake off … itself wake up from sleep (the imitation of death) and look on the real thing

counterfeit imitation

The great doom's image a sight as horrible as the Last Judgement

As from your graves … sprites rise up from your graves and walk like ghosts (continuing the image of the Last Judgement, as it is believed that Christians will rise from their graves on that day)

countenance behold, face

trumpet alarm bell

parley talk with

murder as it fell kill her as she heard it

MACDUFF	Confusion now hath made his masterpiece;
	Most sacrilegious murder hath broke ope 60
	The Lord's anointed temple and stole thence
	The life o'th'building.
MACBETH	What is't you say, the life?
LENNOX	Mean you his majesty?
MACDUFF	Approach the chamber and destroy your sight 65
	With a new Gorgon. Do not bid me speak:
	See and then speak yourselves.

Exeunt Macbeth and Lennox

Awake, awake!
Ring the alarum bell! Murder and treason!
Banquo and Donaldbain! Malcolm, awake,
Shake off this downy sleep, death's counterfeit, 70
And look on death itself. Up, up, and see
The great doom's image. Malcolm, Banquo,
As from your graves rise up and walk like sprites
To countenance this horror.

Bell rings. Enter LADY [MACBETH]

LADY MACBETH	What's the business
	That such a hideous trumpet calls to parley 75
	The sleepers of the house? Speak, speak.
MACDUFF	O gentle lady,
	'Tis not for you to hear what I can speak.
	The repetition in a woman's ear
	Would murder as it fell. –

Enter BANQUO

O Banquo, Banquo,
Our royal master's murdered.

LADY MACBETH	Woe, alas. 80
	What, in our house?
BANQUO	Too cruel, anywhere.
	Dear Duff, I prithee contradict thyself
	And say it is not so.

Language in the play

Is Macbeth sincere? (in pairs)

Look closely at Macbeth's first speech (lines 84–9). Some believe that, in contrast with Macduff's hurried and passionate reaction to finding Duncan's body, Macbeth's words are so carefully constructed and so rich in elaborate imagery that they reveal his insincerity. With a partner, talk about how you would deliver this speech and what you would try to convey to the audience about Macbeth's state of mind.

1 'O, by whom?' (in sevens)

Of the seven characters on stage, only two know who killed Duncan. Take parts and prepare a tableau of line 93 to show just how everyone looks at the moment when Malcolm asks his question. Who is suspicious of whom? Who is making eye contact, and who is avoiding it? Compare the tableaux of each group and discuss why you have made your choices.

Characters

'Look to the lady' (whole class)

Spend some time analysing Macbeth's second, longer, speech. Look at the imagery he uses, as well as the use of devices such as repetition and rhetorical questions. As with lines 84–9, Macbeth seems to have prepared this speech in advance, but behind his words he is justifying another significant murder: that of the only other witnesses to Duncan's killing (he has also taken a long time to announce this shocking news).

a   Why do you think Lady Macbeth faints at this point? Is she sincere? What dramatic purpose does it serve?

b   Discuss how to stage this part of the scene, and experiment by directing a group of volunteers who enact your suggestions. Try the lines without Lady Macbeth fainting. What difference does it make to the effect of the scene?

---

before this chance before this had happened

nothing … mortality nothing important about life any more

toys trivialities, unimportant events

The wine … drawn the sweetness of life has been drained

lees dregs (of a wine glass)

vault world (perhaps with a pun on a wine vault)

brag boast

amiss wrong

The spring, the head the source, the head of the river

your blood your family

stopped blocked

badged marked

distracted confused

Wherefore why

temp'rate calm, restrained

Loyal and neutral loyal to the king and objective about the grooms' guilt

expedition speed or haste

pauser one who hesitates

silver white

golden red

Unmannerly breeched indecently dressed

gore blood

refrain stop himself

Enter MACBETH *and* LENNOX

MACBETH   Had I but died an hour before this chance,
I had lived a blessèd time, for from this instant,   85
There's nothing serious in mortality.
All is but toys; renown and grace is dead,
The wine of life is drawn, and the mere lees
Is left this vault to brag of.

Enter MALCOLM *and* DONALDBAIN

DONALDBAIN What is amiss?

MACBETH   You are, and do not know't.   90
The spring, the head, the fountain of your blood
Is stopped, the very source of it is stopped.

MACDUFF Your royal father's murdered.

MALCOLM   O, by whom?

LENNOX   Those of his chamber, as it seemed, had done't.
Their hands and faces were all badged with blood,   95
So were their daggers which, unwiped, we found
Upon their pillows. They stared and were distracted;
No man's life was to be trusted with them.

MACBETH   O, yet I do repent me of my fury
That I did kill them.

MACDUFF   Wherefore did you so?   100

MACBETH   Who can be wise, amazed, temp'rate, and furious,
Loyal and neutral, in a moment? No man.
Th'expedition of my violent love
Outran the pauser, reason. Here lay Duncan,
His silver skin laced with his golden blood   105
And his gashed stabs looked like a breach in nature,
For ruin's wasteful entrance. There the murderers,
Steeped in the colours of their trade; their daggers
Unmannerly breeched with gore. Who could refrain,
That had a heart to love and in that heart   110
Courage to make's love known?

LADY MACBETH   Help me hence, ho.

MACDUFF Look to the lady.

[Exit Lady Macbeth, helped]

Donaldbain and Malcolm fear for their future. Banquo and the others swear to investigate the murder. Duncan's sons, suspecting danger, resolve to flee: Malcolm to England, Donaldbain to Ireland.

1 Donaldbain and Malcolm: should they stay or should they go? (in pairs)

Should Malcolm and Donaldbain stay in Scotland and find the murderer? Or should they flee? Improvise the arguments for and against each of these actions. Which do you think is the stronger argument? Which is the braver course of action? Do you think they even trust each other now? When considering these arguments, remember that Duncan has already appointed Malcolm as his heir (Act 1 Scene 4, lines 37–8), so he stands to gain most from his father's death. But the younger brother, Donaldbain, has also moved one step closer to the throne with Duncan's death.

2 The qualities of a king

With Malcolm and Donaldbain having fled to England and Ireland respectively, Scotland urgently needs a king. Create a hastily gathered royal court to draw up a job description and outline the qualities the ideal candidate should have. Discuss this as a group and, if you feel strongly about a particular character, argue for them to be crowned king.

Themes
Fate and free will (by yourself)

Imagine you are a psychiatrist. You are faced with characters who seem unable to determine whether it is fate or their own free will that informs their actions. Provide a written report of five key points about one character in Scene 3, telling them what you think is shaping their fate and how they should best respond to this.

Language in the play
Deception and suspicion (in pairs)

The theme of deceptive appearance emerges again in this part of the play, as we see Malcolm and Donaldbain's fearful suspicion of those around them. Present line 133 in the most imaginative way you can, as a tableau, a collection of images or a sketch.

Why do we ... ours? why are we remaining silent when this subject affects us most of all?

auger tiny

tears grief

brewed prepared

upon the foot of motion ready to go, ready to be revealed

naked frailties unclothed bodies or weak feelings

question investigate

scruples doubts

the great hand of God the power of God

undivulged pretence hidden purposes

treasonous malice treacherous hatred, cruel betrayal

briefly quickly

manly readiness our usual clothes; Macbeth could be drawing attention to him being dressed hurriedly, as if from sleep

consort keep company

To show ... easy lying is easy for one who is used to it

Our separated ... safer we'll be safer if we split up

the nea'er in blood ... bloody the more closely related to Duncan, the more likely we are to be killed

shaft arrow

lighted landed, hit its target

dainty of particular about

shift away leave instantly

56

MALCOLM   [*To Donaldbain*] Why do we hold our tongues, that
         most may claim
         This argument for ours?

DONALDBAIN   [*To Malcolm*]   What should be spoken here,
         Where our fate hid in an auger hole may rush   115
         And seize us? Let's away. Our tears are not yet brewed.

MALCOLM   [*To Donaldbain*] Nor our strong sorrow upon the foot
         of motion.

BANQUO   Look to the lady,
         And when we have our naked frailties hid
         That suffer in exposure, let us meet   120
         And question this most bloody piece of work
         To know it further. Fears and scruples shake us:
         In the great hand of God I stand and thence
         Against the undivulged pretence I fight
         Of treasonous malice.

MACDUFF   And so do I.

ALL   So all.   125

MACBETH   Let's briefly put on manly readiness
         And meet i'th'hall together.

ALL   Well contented.
         Exeunt [all but Malcolm and Donaldbain]

MALCOLM   What will you do? Let's not consort with them.
         To show an unfelt sorrow is an office
         Which the false man does easy. I'll to England.   130

DONALDBAIN   To Ireland, I. Our separated fortune
         Shall keep us both the safer. Where we are,
         There's daggers in men's smiles; the nea'er in blood,
         The nearer bloody.

MALCOLM   This murderous shaft that's shot
         Hath not yet lighted, and our safest way   135
         Is to avoid the aim. Therefore to horse,
         And let us not be dainty of leave-taking,
         But shift away. There's warrant in that theft
         Which steals itself when there's no mercy left.
         Exeunt

Stagecraft

The pathetic fallacy

The shocking events taking place inside the castle seem to be mirrored by events in the wider world ("Tis unnatural / Even like the deed that's done'). This use of the **pathetic fallacy** (a literary device used to make the external world seem to be an extension of the moods and actions of the characters) and apocalyptic imagery is intended to create a great impression on the audience. Why do you think Shakespeare uses it here? How successful is it? As you read the rest of the play, add to your notes when you see similar techniques being used.

Characters

Who is the Old Man? (in pairs)

This is the Old Man's only appearance in the play. His dramatic function is rather like the chorus in a Greek tragedy. The role of the chorus was threefold:

- to comment on the action
- to show the universality of the action (how the action is reflected in nature and society)
- to represent the views of ordinary people.

Discuss whether the Old Man fulfils these three roles, then draft a conversation between two people who have different views about the importance of this part of the play. Would you include lines 1–20 in a production at your school?

1 An unimportant scene? (in pairs)

On the surface, the purpose of this scene seems to be simply to inform the audience of recent events. But look closer. Ross is a thane, a high-ranking nobleman, who seems to be mocking an old man. Also, he claims that he saw Duncan's horses eat each other, but do you think this is true? What reason might Ross have for lying about such an event?

Discuss how you would stage this scene to give the two characters more depth and to highlight key themes in the play, such as appearance and reality, the supernatural, hidden evil, and any others that you think are relevant. Write out your ideas as a set of notes to inspire and prompt two actors to bring the script opposite to life as you would want.

Threescore and ten seventy years (a score is twenty)

sore harsh

Hath trifled former knowings has made past events seem trivial

father term of respect for an elderly man

Ha, good father ... it? Ross seems to be speaking cautiously, using figurative language, perhaps testing the Old Man to see where his sympathies lie

heavens/act/stage all terms associated with the theatre

travelling lamp the sun

predominance strong influence

the day's shame Duncan's murder

entomb bury

tow'ring soaring

pride of place at its height, the place where the falcon prides itself in being

mousing owl an owl that swoops to earth to kill mice (rather than rising in the sky to attack birds of prey)

hawked at attacked in flight

minions favourites, the best

Beauteous ... upon't horses, traditionally obedient to man, now seem at war with him; they are attacking and eating each other, suggesting that the natural order of things has broken down

Contending rebelling

good the first time Macduff has been described in this way, contrasting him with Macbeth

How goes the world what is the state of the world?

Act 2 Scene 4
Outside Macbeth's castle

Enter ROSS, *with an* OLD MAN

OLD MAN	Threescore and ten I can remember well;
	Within the volume of which time, I have seen
	Hours dreadful and things strange, but this sore night
	Hath trifled former knowings.
ROSS	Ha, good father,
	Thou seest the heavens, as troubled with man's act,

5

Threatens his bloody stage. By th'clock 'tis day
And yet dark night strangles the travelling lamp.
Is't night's predominance, or the day's shame,
That darkness does the face of earth entomb
When living light should kiss it?

OLD MAN	'Tis unnatural,

10

Even like the deed that's done. On Tuesday last,
A falcon tow'ring in her pride of place
Was by a mousing owl hawked at and killed.

ROSS	And Duncan's horses, a thing most strange and certain,
	Beauteous and swift, the minions of their race,

15

Turned wild in nature, broke their stalls, flung out,
Contending 'gainst obedience as they would
Make war with mankind.

OLD MAN	'Tis said, they eat each other.
ROSS	They did so, to th'amazement of mine eyes
	That looked upon't.

Enter MACDUFF

Here comes the good Macduff.

20

How goes the world, sir, now?

MACDUFF	Why, see you not?

Characters

Macduff: diplomatic or naïve? (in pairs)

This part of the scene is an exposition: it allows the audience to catch up with events that have taken place since the murder of Duncan. Macduff tells us that Duncan's sons bribed the killers and have now fled. He also seems unwilling to comment on the crowning of Macbeth as King of Scotland, although he admits that he is not going to the coronation ceremony.

How does the character of Macduff develop over these twenty lines? With a partner, read through the script opposite. Show by your choice of tone, pace, pause and gesture whether you think Macduff is being diplomatic or naïve, and whether Ross is being deceptive or sincere. Write out your view of each character in a short paragraph.

▼ 'Where the place?' The map below shows the locations of the play. It also shows the rough locations of the territories of the thanes.

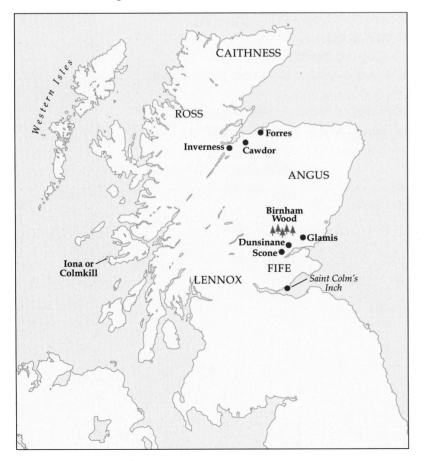

Those that Macbeth hath slain Duncan's guards

pretend give as a reason

suborned bribed (to murder Duncan)

'Gainst nature still the theme of the unnatural continues here

Thriftless ... means the greedy ambition that leads children to kill their own father is self-consuming

ravin up devour greedily

Then ... Macbeth it seems likely that Macbeth will become king

named elected by the thanes; chosen

Scone palace near Perth where kings of Scotland were crowned

invested crowned ceremonially

Colmkill Iona, the traditional burial place of Scottish kings

Fife Scottish county; Macduff's ancestral territory

I will thither I will go there

Lest our old robes ... new in case the future is less comfortable than the past

benison blessing

ROSS	Is't known who did this more than bloody deed?
MACDUFF	Those that Macbeth hath slain.
ROSS	Alas the day,
	What good could they pretend?

ROSS   Alas the day,
What good could they pretend?

MACDUFF   They were suborned.
Malcolm and Donaldbain, the king's two sons,   25
Are stol'n away and fled, which puts upon them
Suspicion of the deed.

ROSS   'Gainst nature still.
Thriftless ambition that will ravin up
Thine own life's means. Then 'tis most like
The sovereignty will fall upon Macbeth.   30

MACDUFF He is already named and gone to Scone
To be invested.

ROSS Where is Duncan's body?

MACDUFF   Carried to Colmkill,
The sacred storehouse of his predecessors
And guardian of their bones.

ROSS   Will you to Scone?   35

MACDUFF No, cousin, I'll to Fife.

ROSS   Well, I will thither.

MACDUFF Well may you see things well done there. Adieu,
Lest our old robes sit easier than our new.

ROSS Farewell, father.

OLD MAN God's benison go with you, and with those   40
That would make good of bad, and friends of foes.

                                              Exeunt

Looking back at Act 2
Activities for groups or individuals

1 'the bloody business'

Blood is a recurring symbol throughout *Macbeth*, but in Act 2, with the murder of Duncan, it is used particularly vividly. Find all the images of blood in Act 2 and consider the different ways it is represented. You could act out each section, or create tableaux of the most powerful lines in groups.

2 Storyboarding the main action

Act 2 moves at real pace. Storyboard the main points of action: which scenes will you choose, and what lines will you select to illustrate each image? What will you decide to leave out, and why? Put each image together into a continuous sequence, either using pen and paper, or a computer with a film-editing program.

3 A favourite speech

This act has many powerful speeches. Choose your favourite (between ten and twenty lines) and set yourself the challenge of learning those lines. Think about the rhythm, the stresses, the tone and the meaning you wish to convey. Try filming your interpretation of these lines and then show your work to the rest of your class. Discuss the decisions you made in building your performance.

4 Thinking about the big themes

Working by yourself, make a list of what you consider to be the main themes in Act 2. When you have your list, get together with the rest of your class. Each person should explain their choices. Together, agree on the five most important themes in this act.

Next, take five large pieces of paper and write one key theme in the middle of each piece. Split into five groups and take one piece of paper each. Discuss the theme on your piece of paper for five minutes, writing down your thoughts. At the end of five minutes, pass on your piece of paper and move on to the next theme, writing down your thoughts and responding to those that the previous groups have written down. Keep going until each group has considered all five themes. Afterwards, keep these pieces of paper and add to them as you continue to work through the rest of the play.

If you wanted to continue this activity, you could explore an additional area: the link between themes. For example, you could investigate the connections between the themes of loyalty and ambition, conscience and action.

5 Macbeth: hero or villain?

At the end of Act 2, it is possible to see the character of Macbeth in a number of different ways:

- He is a heartless killer who has murdered a kind king purely for his own benefit.
- He is politically clever and acts ruthlessly simply because he lives in ruthless times.
- He is easily manipulated by a wife he loves, and acts to prove to her that he is a man.
- He has no choice: the Witches told him what was going to happen and it was fated to be so.
- He is a hero who has been selected by the thanes to rescue Scotland in its hour of need.

Which of these interpretations do you think is the most valid? Write down your reasons, using quotations where appropriate. Now list them in order of priority and debate your choices with each other. Can you think of any other ways to see Macbeth at this point in the play?

Banquo fears that Macbeth has become king by evil means, but he takes heart from the Witches' predictions for his own descendants. Macbeth requests Banquo to attend tonight's banquet.

1 Noble Banquo?

Initially, Banquo – like Macbeth – dwells on the words of the Witches. His thoughts are interrupted by the entrance of Macbeth and Lady Macbeth.

a Was he saying 'hush, no more' to rebuke the thoughts that might have led him to evil, or so that the Macbeths would not hear him? What might he have said if he had carried on? Compose an extension to this aside to reveal Banquo's thoughts and feelings further.

b How would you enact lines 15–18? Would Banquo be noble and sincere or hypocritical and deceptive? Experiment with ways of saying these lines aloud, varying the emphasis and intonation to reveal different meanings.

▼ Macbeth now wears the crown of Scotland, but what does his face reveal about his 'mind's construction'?

stand in thy posterity remain in your family

father / Of many kings according to popular legend, King James I (and VI of Scotland) was a descendant of Banquo

verities truths

made good proved

oracles prophets

Sennet trumpet call (of seven notes)

all thing unbecoming totally inappropriate or unacceptable

Command upon me I am at your disposal

Act 3 Scene 1
The royal palace at Forres

Enter BANQUO *dressed for riding*

BANQUO   Thou hast it now, King, Cawdor, Glamis, all,
As the weïrd women promised, and I fear
Thou played'st most foully for't; yet it was said
It should not stand in thy posterity,
But that myself should be the root and father   5
Of many kings. If there come truth from them –
As upon thee, Macbeth, their speeches shine –
Why by the verities on thee made good,
May they not be my oracles as well
And set me up in hope? But hush, no more.   10

Sennet sounded. Enter MACBETH *as King,* LADY [MACBETH *as*
Queen], LENNOX, ROSS, *Lords, and Attendants*

MACBETH   Here's our chief guest.

LADY MACBETH   If he had been forgotten,
It had been as a gap in our great feast
And all thing unbecoming.

MACBETH   Tonight we hold a solemn supper, sir,
And I'll request your presence.

BANQUO   Let your highness   15
Command upon me, to the which my duties
Are with a most indissoluble tie
Forever knit.

Macbeth claims that Duncan's sons are spreading malicious rumours. He checks that Fleance will ride this afternoon with Banquo, then dismisses the court. A servant confirms two men (the Murderers) are waiting.

Themes

Hidden evil (in pairs)

Macbeth flatters Banquo as a valued adviser. He pretends to be interested in Banquo's ride that afternoon, but in his heart Macbeth has evil intentions for his friend. His order 'Fail not our feast' is deeply ironic, because Macbeth intends that Banquo will never return from his ride.

With a partner, read slowly all Macbeth's words in lines 19–41. As one person reads, the other says 'false face' or 'hypocrite' every time he says something insincere. At each point, give a reason why Macbeth is false, or describe what is really on his mind.

1 'strange invention' (by yourself)

Malcolm has escaped to England and Donaldbain to Ireland. Macbeth accuses them of influencing the king and people there with tales of 'strange invention'. Step into role as either Malcolm or Donaldbain. Write your side of the story in the form of a speech to be delivered to the people of England or Ireland (or any other country) who might support your cause. Why have you not confessed to 'cruel parricide' and what do you intend to do to clear your name?

Characters

Why is Lady Macbeth dismissed? (in pairs)

In many productions, Lady Macbeth approaches Macbeth at line 45, obviously wanting to talk to him, but is dismissed with everyone else when he says 'While then, God be with you'. Does Macbeth send his wife away because the evil they have committed is beginning to drive them apart? Or is Macbeth just distracted by his plans for getting rid of Banquo?

With a partner, improvise the conversation that might have taken place between Macbeth and Lady Macbeth if they were left on stage together at this point.

---

still always

grave serious or important

prosperous successful, fortunate

take tomorrow command your attendance tomorrow

'Twixt this between now

Go not my horse the better if my horse isn't speedy

borrower of the night traveller who must extend his journey into the night hours

twain two

bloody bloodstained, murdering

cousins Malcolm and Donaldbain

parricide murder of their father

strange invention lies, rumours

therewithal with it also

Craving us jointly requiring the attention of both of us

Hie you hurry

master of his time responsible for his own activities

While until

Sirrah form of address to a social inferior

those men the Murderers

without outside

MACBETH	Ride you this afternoon?
BANQUO	Ay, my good lord. 20
MACBETH	We should have else desired your good advice
	Which still hath been both grave and prosperous
	In this day's council: but we'll take tomorrow.
	Is't far you ride?
BANQUO	As far, my lord, as will fill up the time 25
	'Twixt this and supper. Go not my horse the better,
	I must become a borrower of the night
	For a dark hour, or twain.
MACBETH	Fail not our feast.
BANQUO	My lord, I will not. 30
MACBETH	We hear our bloody cousins are bestowed
	In England and in Ireland, not confessing
	Their cruel parricide, filling their hearers
	With strange invention. But of that tomorrow,
	When therewithal we shall have cause of state 35
	Craving us jointly. Hie you to horse; adieu,
	Till you return at night. Goes Fleance with you?
BANQUO	Ay, my good lord; our time does call upon's.
MACBETH	I wish your horses swift and sure of foot,
	And so I do commend you to their backs. 40
	Farewell.

Exit Banquo

Let every man be master of his time
Till seven at night; to make society
The sweeter welcome, we will keep ourself
Till supper-time alone. While then, God be with you.   45

Exeunt [all but Macbeth and a Servant]

Sirrah, a word with you: attend those men
Our pleasure?

SERVANT	They are, my lord, without the palace gate.

1 Thoughts of Banquo (in pairs)

As he waits for the Murderers, Macbeth reveals how much he fears Banquo. Interestingly, while he earlier acted to ensure that the Witches' prophecy would come true (so he could be king), he now takes steps to ensure their prophecy for Banquo's descendants will *not* come true.

To experience how much Macbeth now fears Banquo, read through the soliloquy while your partner echoes any word referring to Banquo (his name, 'he', 'his', 'him') in an angry voice, and any word referring to Macbeth ('I', 'my', 'me') in a complaining voice.

Language in the play
Fruitless and barren (in pairs)

Macbeth speaks bitterly of the 'fruitless crown' and 'barren sceptre' that the Witches have given him. He is jealous of Banquo because of the prophecy that Banquo will be 'father to a line of kings'.

a   With a partner, draw up a list of images or phrases that signify fruitfulness or honour for Banquo, and those that suggest barrenness and dishonour for Macbeth. Talk together about which image is the most striking. Why is this so?

b   Write two short paragraphs: one on Macbeth's use of language and the other on the insight it gives into his mental state. Swap your paragraphs with your partner and compare your perspectives. Are they the same?

---

2 'our last conference' (in threes)

Macbeth had an earlier meeting with the Murderers. He told them ('passed in probation with you') that Banquo had deceived them ('borne in hand'), and it was all Banquo's doing that they were so poor and out of luck ('held you so under fortune').

Improvise that earlier conversation as Macbeth lays all the blame on Banquo. Take lines 77–83 and 85–9 as your starting point and use either modern English or blank verse in the style of Shakespeare.

---

thus king

dauntless fearless

being existence
genius guardian angel
chid challenged, rebuked

gripe grasp
wrenched twisted or dislocated
with an unlineal hand by someone not of my family
issue descendants
filed defiled or polluted
rancours bitterness, poison
vessel cup
eternal jewel immortal soul
common enemy enemy of all people: Satan
seeds descendants
list jousting tournament, battlefield
champion me to th'utterance challenge me to the furthest limit (death)

he Banquo
conference discussion
passed in probation proved
borne in hand deceived or misled
crossed double-crossed
half a soul half-wit or idiot
notion mind

MACBETH   Bring them before us.

Exit Servant

To be thus is nothing,
But to be safely thus. Our fears in Banquo   50
Stick deep, and in his royalty of nature
Reigns that which would be feared. 'Tis much he dares,
And to that dauntless temper of his mind,
He hath a wisdom that doth guide his valour
To act in safety. There is none but he,   55
Whose being I do fear; and under him
My genius is rebuked, as it is said
Mark Antony's was by Caesar. He chid the sisters
When first they put the name of king upon me
And bade them speak to him. Then prophet-like,   60
They hailed him father to a line of kings.
Upon my head they placed a fruitless crown
And put a barren sceptre in my gripe,
Thence to be wrenched with an unlineal hand,
No son of mine succeeding. If't be so,   65
For Banquo's issue have I filed my mind;
For them, the gracious Duncan have I murdered,
Put rancours in the vessel of my peace
Only for them, and mine eternal jewel
Given to the common enemy of man,   70
To make them kings, the seeds of Banquo kings.
Rather than so, come Fate into the list,
And champion me to th'utterance. Who's there?

Enter Servant and two MURDERERS

[*To Servant*] Now go to the door and stay there till we call.

Exit Servant

Was it not yesterday we spoke together?   75
MURDERERS   It was, so please your highness.
MACBETH Well then, now have you considered of my speeches?
Know, that it was he in the times past which held you so under
fortune, which you thought had been our innocent self. This I
made good to you in our last conference; passed in probation   80
with you how you were borne in hand, how crossed; the instruments, who wrought with them, and all things else that might to
half a soul and to a notion crazed say, 'Thus did Banquo.'

Macbeth taunts the Murderers, urging them to show they are men, not dogs. If they can prove their manhood, he will help them to kill Banquo. The Murderers claim that they are so desperate they'll do anything.

Write about it

Men and dogs

Earlier in the play, Lady Macbeth questioned Macbeth's manhood in an attempt to manipulate him into murdering Duncan. Now Macbeth does the same thing with the Murderers. He describes a variety of dogs ('Shoughs', 'water-rugs', 'demi-wolves') and lists their different qualities ('swift', 'slow', 'subtle'). He suggests that men can similarly be ranked by their qualities. As he does this, Macbeth shifts from prose to verse at line 91. Convert the prose to verse, and the verse to prose. What difference does it make?

1 Murder and manipulation (in small groups)

Prepare a dramatic reading of the script opposite. Use the following questions to help you:

- Would Macbeth be seated while the Murderers stand, or would all stand?
- Would Macbeth remain hidden in the shadows or would he tower above the Murderers?
- Would he have freedom of movement and a wide vocal range to show his power over the Murderers, who fearfully stay in one place on the stage?
- Would the Murderers be restless, wild and violent men who gradually become subject to Macbeth's manipulation?

so gospelled such believers in the Christian doctrine of forgiving your enemies

yours your families

catalogue list

clept called

valued file list with values or qualities attached

housekeeper watchdog

closed enclosed

Particular addition a specific mark of distinction

bill list, label

station in the file place in the list of valued people (or soldiers)

rank sort, level

put that ... bosoms reveal a plan to you

execution carrying out, doing

takes ... off removes or kills

Grapples attaches firmly

in his life while he lives

perfect excellent

tugged with mauled by

set my life on gamble my life on

on't of it

70

FIRST MURDERER   You made it known to us.

MACBETH I did so, and went further, which is now our point of   85
second meeting. Do you find your patience so predominant in
your nature, that you can let this go? Are you so gospelled, to
pray for this good man and for his issue, whose heavy hand
hath bowed you to the grave and beggared yours forever?

FIRST MURDERER   We are men, my liege.   90

MACBETH   Ay, in the catalogue ye go for men,
As hounds, and greyhounds, mongrels, spaniels, curs,
Shoughs, water-rugs, and demi-wolves are clept
All by the name of dogs. The valued file
Distinguishes the swift, the slow, the subtle,   95
The housekeeper, the hunter, every one
According to the gift which bounteous nature
Hath in him closed, whereby he does receive
Particular addition from the bill
That writes them all alike. And so of men.   100
Now, if you have a station in the file
Not i'th'worst rank of manhood, say't,
And I will put that business in your bosoms,
Whose execution takes your enemy off,
Grapples you to the heart and love of us   105
Who wear our health but sickly in his life,
Which in his death were perfect.

SECOND MURDERER   I am one, my liege,
Whom the vile blows and buffets of the world
Hath so incensed that I am reckless what I do
To spite the world.

FIRST MURDERER   And I another,   110
So weary with disasters, tugged with fortune,
That I would set my life on any chance
To mend it or be rid on't.

MACBETH   Both of you know
Banquo was your enemy.

MURDERERS   True, my lord.

Macbeth says that Banquo is his enemy, but he cannot kill him openly. He will arrange a time and place for the Murderers to assassinate Banquo and Fleance, so that no suspicion falls upon himself.

Stagecraft

A tyrant and his thugs

Like all tyrants, Macbeth hires thugs and villains to do his dirty work for him. Note that Macbeth does not simply order the Murderers to kill Banquo, but gives them reasons for his orders and takes them into his confidence.

a Read the script again and identify where Macbeth seems to relate to the Murderers in ways that are:

- friendly and confidential
- anxious
- threatening
- contemptuous or dismissive.

b Explore ways of staging this part of the script for a modern production, taking into account the factors below and trying out some of the movements or gestures you would want the actors to use:

- Stage space – how would the actors exploit this?
- Lighting – how would the stage be lit to emphasise the intensity of this manipulation scene?
- Sound effects – what music or other sounds would you use here?
- Movement, expressions and gestures – experiment with these to characterise Macbeth and the Murderers.

Language in the play

Killing the killers (in pairs)

Macbeth's last two lines before he has Banquo murdered (140–1) are in the form of a rhyming couplet. His last two lines before murdering Duncan are in the same form (Act 2 Scene 1, lines 63–4).

a Write out these two sets of rhyming couplets. Why do you think Shakespeare used this device to craft Macbeth's language before the death of two significant characters?

b Imagine that Macbeth intends to kill the two Murderers after they have murdered Banquo. Write a rhyming couplet of your own, revealing Macbeth's intention to kill the killers.

---

distance enmity, quarrel (distance between swordsmen)

near'st of life very existence

barefaced naked or open

bid my will avouch it justify it by my desires

but wail but I must appear to mourn

make love pay close attention

common eye public view

plant position

perfect spy o'th'time exact information

something from away from

always ... clearness remember that I must be free from suspicion

rubs nor botches flaws or bungling

absence death, murder

material important

Resolve ... apart decide between yourselves who will kill Banquo and who will kill Fleance

anon soon

straight at once

thy soul's flight your death (this was imagined as a bird that could escape the body and fly to heaven or hell)

MACBETH So is he mine, and in such bloody distance   115
That every minute of his being thrusts
Against my near'st of life; and though I could
With barefaced power sweep him from my sight
And bid my will avouch it, yet I must not,
For certain friends that are both his and mine,   120
Whose loves I may not drop, but wail his fall
Who I myself struck down. And thence it is
That I to your assistance do make love,
Masking the business from the common eye
For sundry weighty reasons.

SECOND MURDERER   We shall, my lord,   125
Perform what you command us.

FIRST MURDERER   Though our lives –

MACBETH Your spirits shine through you. Within this hour at most,
I will advise you where to plant yourselves,
Acquaint you with the perfect spy o'th'time,
The moment on't, for't must be done tonight,   130
And something from the palace: always thought,
That I require a clearness. And with him,
To leave no rubs nor botches in the work,
Fleance, his son that keeps him company,
Whose absence is no less material to me   135
Than is his father's, must embrace the fate
Of that dark hour. Resolve yourselves apart,
I'll come to you anon.

MURDERERS   We are resolved, my lord.

MACBETH I'll call upon you straight; abide within.

                                        [*Exeunt Murderers*]

It is concluded. Banquo, thy soul's flight,   140
If it find heaven, must find it out tonight.   *Exit*

Lady Macbeth is troubled. She advises Macbeth not to brood on what's done, but he is still racked by fears and insecurity. He even envies the peace of death that Duncan enjoys.

1 Apocalyptic dreams (in pairs)

This scene marks a change in the relationship between Macbeth and Lady Macbeth. Both are uneasy about their present position: Lady Macbeth says 'Nought's had, all's spent' and Macbeth is full of 'sorriest fancies'. However, Lady Macbeth's advice to her husband is simply to forget the events of the past because they cannot be changed – 'what's done, is done'.

a Identify some of the reasons Macbeth gives about why it is impossible for him to forget the past. Improvise a scenario in which Macbeth unburdens his mind more fully. Imagine him on a psychoanalyst's couch, telling of the terrible dreams that torment him and giving a truthful account of everything that is troubling him (lines 13–26).

b Study the photograph below. Pick out lines from this scene that could make a suitable caption.

Nought's had, all's spent nothing's gained, everything's lost

sorriest fancies miserable visions

what's done, is done proverb: 'what is done cannot be undone'

scorched slashed

close, and be herself heal and join together again

poor malice weak deed (the murder of Duncan)

let the frame of things disjoint let the universe shatter

both the worlds suffer Earth and heaven be destroyed

lie / In restless ecstasy lie as on an instrument of torture (the rack)

sleeps well sleeps the peaceful, eternal sleep of death

Malice domestic civil war

foreign levy foreign armies

Act 3 Scene 2
A room in Macbeth's palace

Enter LADY MACBETH, *and a* SERVANT

LADY MACBETH Is Banquo gone from court?

SERVANT Ay, madam, but returns again tonight.

LADY MACBETH Say to the king, I would attend his leisure
For a few words.

SERVANT   Madam, I will.   *Exit*

LADY MACBETH   Nought's had, all's spent
Where our desire is got without content.   5
'Tis safer to be that which we destroy
Than by destruction dwell in doubtful joy.

Enter MACBETH

How now, my lord, why do you keep alone,
Of sorriest fancies your companions making,
Using those thoughts which should indeed have died   10
With them they think on? Things without all remedy
Should be without regard; what's done, is done.

MACBETH We have scorched the snake, not killed it;
She'll close, and be herself, whilst our poor malice
Remains in danger of her former tooth.   15
But let the frame of things disjoint, both the worlds suffer,
Ere we will eat our meal in fear, and sleep
In the affliction of these terrible dreams
That shake us nightly. Better be with the dead
Whom we, to gain our peace, have sent to peace,   20
Than on the torture of the mind to lie
In restless ecstasy. Duncan is in his grave.
After life's fitful fever, he sleeps well;
Treason has done his worst; nor steel nor poison,
Malice domestic, foreign levy, nothing   25
Can touch him further.

Macbeth tells his wife to pay special regard to Banquo at the banquet. He speaks contemptuously of having to flatter deceitfully. He hints darkly that terrible deeds will be performed that night.

1 Statement and replies (whole class)

Stand in a circle around one student, who is going to address different people in the circle with a 'statement' from the script opposite. He or she (in role as Lady Macbeth or Macbeth) should walk up to various people in the circle to say the line and hear their response. If you are standing in the circle, you should memorise the 'reply' so that you can say it in response with your choice of intonation, emotion, volume and accompanying gestures. Try both statements below, then find other lines from the play to experiment with in this way.

- Statement: You must leave this.
  Reply: O, full of scorpions is my mind, dear wife!
- Statement: What's to be done?
  Reply: Be innocent of the knowledge, dearest chuck

Language in the play

Scorpions, bats, beetles and crows (in pairs)

Shakespeare uses animal imagery for sinister and dramatic effect in lines 36–53. For example, a bat is a creature that fulfils Hecate's orders. The words 'seeling' and 'scarf' relate to falconry, where the falconer would temporarily blind the hawk so that it would remain dependent on him until it was fully trained. List the animals mentioned and describe the roles they have in the creation of a chillingly dark atmosphere in this part of the scene.

Write about it

Close reading (by yourself)

Macbeth's language in lines 46–50 is rich and visceral in its personification of night and day. It evokes vivid images of blood and blindness, evil and darkness, adding to the drama of the scene.

a What effect does Macbeth's strikingly poetic language have when contrasted with the sinister atmosphere created by his invocation to evil? Write a paragraph describing the impact of Macbeth's language, using embedded quotations as you refer to the script opposite.

b In role as either Macbeth or Lady Macbeth, write about your thoughts and feelings in a secret diary at the end of this scene.

Sleek smooth

rugged furrowed or wrinkled

remembrance thought or regard

present him eminence praise and honour him

unsafe the while it's still a dangerous time for us

lave wash

vizards masks

Nature's copy's not eterne life doesn't last for ever

assailable vulnerable to attack

jocund merry or cheerful

shard-born born in dung

Be innocent … deed don't worry in advance about an event that you will welcome when it is done

chuck affectionate nickname derived from 'chick'

seeling blinding (hawks' eyes were 'seeled' by sewing them up)

Scarf up blindfold

bond moral obligation

Light thickens it grows dark

makes wing flies

rooky filled with rooks

hold thee still continue steadfast as you have been

76

LADY MACBETH   Come on. Gentle my lord,
Sleek o'er your rugged looks, be bright and jovial
Among your guests tonight.

MACBETH   So shall I, love,
And so I pray be you. Let your remembrance   30
Apply to Banquo, present him eminence
Both with eye and tongue; unsafe the while, that we
Must lave our honours in these flattering streams
And make our faces vizards to our hearts,
Disguising what they are.

LADY MACBETH   You must leave this.   35

MACBETH   O, full of scorpions is my mind, dear wife!
Thou know'st that Banquo and his Fleance lives.

LADY MACBETH   But in them Nature's copy's not eterne.

MACBETH   There's comfort yet, they are assailable;
Then be thou jocund: ere the bat hath flown   40
His cloistered flight, ere to black Hecate's summons
The shard-born beetle with his drowsy hums
Hath rung night's yawning peal, there shall be done
A deed of dreadful note.

LADY MACBETH   What's to be done?

MACBETH   Be innocent of the knowledge, dearest chuck,   45
Till thou applaud the deed. Come, seeling night,
Scarf up the tender eye of pitiful day
And with thy bloody and invisible hand
Cancel and tear to pieces that great bond
Which keeps me pale. Light thickens,   50
And the crow makes wing to th'rooky wood;
Good things of day begin to droop and drowse,
Whiles night's black agents to their preys do rouse.
Thou marvell'st at my words, but hold thee still;
Things bad begun, make strong themselves by ill.   55
So prithee, go with me.

                                        Exeunt

Stagecraft

Hidden clues (in small groups)

Shakespeare's stage was quite bare and the actors didn't have time to rehearse the play in detail (see 'Macbeth in performance', pp. 174).

a Read the script opposite and look for clues that Shakespeare gives the actors for internal stage directions (information about what to do on stage). Look out also for lines that help the audience imagine what is happening on the stage. Copy the table below and fill it in, adding further examples.

Quotation	Action for actor	Imagination for audience
'But who did bid thee join with us?' (line 1)	A third actor walks on stage	
'The west yet glimmers with some streaks of day' (line 5)		It is twilight and nearly dark
'Hark, I hear horses.' (line 8)		
'A light, a light!' (line 15)		
'Stand to't.' (line 17)		

b How would you direct this murder scene for a new movie production set in your school? Think about the people you would cast, music for the score, set and props, use of camera angles and special effects.

c Write out your ideas for filming this scene, or create a storyboard. In groups, have a go at filming the section, then hold a screening session in class to review everyone's version of the scene.

offices duties
To the direction just precisely

spurs the lated gallops the late
timely opportune
The subject of our watch the person we are waiting for

within the note of expectation on the list of expected guests

go about turn back

Make it their walk Banquo and Fleance walk almost a mile to the castle while the grooms cool their horses

best half of our affair half our reward (or half our task)

Act 3 Scene 3
A lonely place near Forres

Enter three MURDERERS

FIRST MURDERER   But who did bid thee join with us?

THIRD MURDERER   Macbeth.

SECOND MURDERER   He needs not our mistrust, since he delivers
    Our offices and what we have to do
    To the direction just.

FIRST MURDERER   [*To Third Murderer*] Then stand with us.
    The west yet glimmers with some streaks of day;   5
    Now spurs the lated traveller apace
    To gain the timely inn, and near approaches
    The subject of our watch.

THIRD MURDERER   Hark, I hear horses.

BANQUO   (*Within*) Give us a light there, ho!

SECOND MURDERER   Then 'tis he; the rest
    That are within the note of expectation   10
    Already are i'th'court.

FIRST MURDERER   His horses go about.

THIRD MURDERER   Almost a mile; but he does usually,
    So all men do, from hence to th'palace gate
    Make it their walk.

Enter BANQUO *and* FLEANCE, *with a torch*

SECOND MURDERER   A light, a light!   15

THIRD MURDERER   'Tis he.

FIRST MURDERER   Stand to't.

BANQUO   It will be rain tonight.

FIRST MURDERER   Let it come down.
    [*The Murderers attack. First Murderer strikes out the light*]

BANQUO   O, treachery!
    Fly, good Fleance, fly, fly, fly!   20
    Thou mayst revenge – O slave!   [*Dies. Fleance escapes*]

THIRD MURDERER   Who did strike out the light?

FIRST MURDERER   Was't not the way?

THIRD MURDERER   There's but one down; the son is fled.

SECOND MURDERER   We have lost best half of our affair.

FIRST MURDERER   Well, let's away, and say how much is done.   25
    Exeunt[, with Banquo's body]

Macbeth welcomes his guests to the banquet and mixes with them. The First Murderer reports Banquo's death. The news of Fleance's escape disturbs Macbeth and renews his fears.

Themes
The humble host? (in pairs)

False and deceptive behaviour recurs throughout the play, contributing to the theme of appearance and reality.

a How does Macbeth create the appearance of peace and harmony at the beginning of this scene? How is this undercut by the presence of the Murderers, who have secret instructions from the king?

b Macbeth avoids naming the deed (murder). Listen to the difference it makes when you read his lines to the Murderer and substitute 'kill' or 'murder' for Macbeth's evasive language.

c List four euphemisms for murder that Macbeth uses in his conversation with the Murderer (lines 15–28). Describe how they relate to the theme of appearance and reality.

1 Stark contrasts (in pairs or small groups)

Macbeth uses stark contrasts to express his disappointment that Fleance has escaped (lines 21–5). Read these lines and work with a partner or a group to create a tableau of each of the two images Macbeth describes. Switch from one to the other to show the difference between appearance and reality – and to demonstrate Macbeth's fears for the future – as you present your tableaux to the class.

Stagecraft
'Is he dispatched?'

Macbeth's place at the banqueting table is in the middle among his guests. He plans to 'drink a measure / The table round', but first leaves to talk to the Murderers.

Imagine you are an audience member at a performance that has just played this scene well, allowing the audience to hear the conversation between Macbeth and the Murderer, but not the guests at the banquet. How was this conversation staged? What effect might this scene have on an audience if staged the way you imagine it?

---

your own degrees the seating order appropriate to your status

society acquaintances
keeps her state stays on her throne

large unrestrained
measure toast

better thee … within better on the outside of you than on the inside of Banquo

the nonpareil without equal

fit anxiety
founded secure, immovable
As broad and general secure and free
casing surrounding
cribbed shut in a tiny space
saucy distressing
safe dead
trenchèd furrowed or gaping
least smallest one

Act 3 Scene 4
The banqueting hall at Forres

Banquet prepared. Two thrones are placed on stage. Enter MACBETH *as King,* LADY MACBETH *as Queen,* ROSS, LENNOX, LORDS, *and attendants. Lady Macbeth sits*

MACBETH You know your own degrees, sit down; at first and last, the hearty welcome.

[The Lords sit]

LORDS Thanks to your majesty.

MACBETH Our self will mingle with society and play the humble host; our hostess keeps her state, but in best time we will require her welcome. 5

LADY MACBETH Pronounce it for me, sir, to all our friends, for my heart speaks, they are welcome.

Enter FIRST MURDERER

MACBETH See, they encounter thee with their hearts' thanks.
Both sides are even; here I'll sit i'th'midst. 10
Be large in mirth, anon we'll drink a measure
The table round. [*To First Murderer*] There's blood upon thy face.

FIRST MURDERER 'Tis Banquo's then.

MACBETH 'Tis better thee without, than he within.
Is he dispatched? 15

FIRST MURDERER My lord, his throat is cut; that I did for him.

MACBETH Thou art the best o'th'cut-throats,
Yet he's good that did the like for Fleance;
If thou didst it, thou art the nonpareil.

FIRST MURDERER Most royal sir, Fleance is scaped. 20

MACBETH Then comes my fit again: I had else been perfect;
Whole as the marble, founded as the rock,
As broad and general as the casing air:
But now I am cabined, cribbed, confined, bound in
To saucy doubts and fears. But Banquo's safe? 25

FIRST MURDERER Ay, my good lord: safe in a ditch he bides,
With twenty trenchèd gashes on his head,
The least a death to nature.

Macbeth consoles himself that Fleance is too young to do harm yet. Lady Macbeth bids him welcome his guests. The sight of Banquo's Ghost unnerves Macbeth. Lady Macbeth attempts to calm the Lords.

Stagecraft

Ghost or no ghost? (in pairs)

Every time *Macbeth* is performed, the director must decide whether or not to bring on a Ghost that the audience can see, or whether to leave it to the audience's imagination. On Shakespeare's stage, an actor was made up with animal blood and possibly with flour to give him a deathly white complexion. With a partner, decide how you would stage the scene in a theatre production. Would your Ghost be visible or invisible? Why? Explain your decision to the class, then take a vote.

Write about it

Dramatic irony

The appearance of Banquo's Ghost on stage gives much opportunity for dramatic irony, and there are several points where the audience is more aware of what is happening than the characters are.

a Look at the following quotations from the script and give at least two versions of what the statement might mean:
  • Macbeth: 'Sweet remembrancer!' (line 37)
  • Macbeth: 'Here had we now our country's honour roofed, / Were the graced person of our Banquo present' (lines 40–1)
  • Ross: 'His absence, sir, / Lays blame upon his promise' (lines 43–4)
  • Macbeth: 'Which of you have done this?' (line 49). Remember, Macbeth is not aware that no one else can see the Ghost. His question assumes that this is a practical joke.

b Write three or four paragraphs describing how the Ghost adds to the horror and intrigue in this scene, as well as contributing to its dramatic irony.

grown serpent Banquo

worm Fleance (figuratively, a larva or grub that will grow into a venomous snake)

hear ourselves speak together

give the cheer welcome your guests

is sold … without it unless there are many ceremonious welcomes, it's like a take-away meal

To feed … home one dines best in one's own dwelling

From thence away from home

ceremony social rituals of seating, serving, toasting

remembrancer one who reminds

wait on attend or serve

honour nobility

graced favoured

Who may … mischance I hope he's absent because of unkindness rather than an accident

His absence … promise Banquo's absence breaks his promise to attend

The table's full Macbeth cannot find an empty place at the table

moves troubles (Macbeth has reacted to the Ghost)

gory locks blood-covered hair

keep seat remain seated

fit seizure

upon a thought in a moment (proverb: 'as swift as thought')

If much you note him if you watch him closely

passion fit

82

MACBETH   Thanks for that.
There the grown serpent lies; the worm that's fled
Hath nature that in time will venom breed,   30
No teeth for th'present. Get thee gone; tomorrow
We'll hear ourselves again,

                                    Exit [First] Murderer

LADY MACBETH   My royal lord,
You do not give the cheer; the feast is sold
That is not often vouched while 'tis a-making,
'Tis given with welcome. To feed were best at home: 35
From thence, the sauce to meat is ceremony,
Meeting were bare without it.

          Enter the Ghost of Banquo and sits in Macbeth's place

MACBETH   Sweet remembrancer!
Now good digestion wait on appetite,
And health on both.

LENNOX   May't please your highness, sit.

MACBETH   Here had we now our country's honour roofed,   40
Were the graced person of our Banquo present,
Who may I rather challenge for unkindness
Than pity for mischance.

ROSS   His absence, sir,
Lays blame upon his promise. Please't your highness
To grace us with your royal company?   45

MACBETH   The table's full.

LENNOX   Here is a place reserved, sir.

MACBETH   Where?

LENNOX   Here, my good lord. What is't that moves your highness?

MACBETH   Which of you have done this?

LORDS   What, my good lord?

MACBETH   Thou canst not say I did it; never shake   50
Thy gory locks at me!

ROSS   Gentlemen, rise, his highness is not well.

                    [Lady Macbeth joins the Lords]

LADY MACBETH   Sit, worthy friends. My lord is often thus,
And hath been from his youth. Pray you, keep seat.
The fit is momentary; upon a thought   55
He will again be well. If much you note him
You shall offend him and extend his passion.
Feed, and regard him not. *[To Macbeth]* Are you a man?

Lady Macbeth rebukes Macbeth for his display of fear. The Ghost leaves. Macbeth broods on how the dead return. He recovers his composure, reassures the thanes and proposes a toast. The Ghost re-enters.

Characters

'O proper stuff!'

Lady Macbeth ridicules and insults Macbeth in an attempt to get him to come to his senses. Practise reading lines 60–8 with as much disgust as possible. Take note of her short sentences, rhetorical question and references to horror stories told by old women. What do you think is the most devastating aspect of her outburst? What effect do you think it has on Macbeth?

Stagecraft

Staging the banquet (in pairs)

How would you advise the actors in this scene? Imagine you are a director and you want to explore ways of using stage space, gesture, pitch and pace. Create a stage plan on A3 paper and include a page of written instructions to the actors. Remember to look at the clues Shakespeare has given in the internal stage directions (especially lines 67, 70 and 88). Give particular attention to the following:

- the secret conversation between Lady Macbeth and Macbeth (lines 59–73)
- the Ghost's exit (line 73)
- Macbeth's horror (expressed either to himself or to Lady Macbeth in lines 75–83)
- Macbeth's awareness of his guests and their reactions (remember that no one else can see the Ghost)
- the re-entry of the Ghost just as Macbeth proposes the toast he promised at the beginning of the scene (line 88)

Swap and compare your stage plan and instructions with another pair, then evaluate the most effective way of staging this scene.

---

proper stuff complete or utter nonsense

painting image or illusion

air-drawn imagined

dagger ... Duncan Lady Macbeth ridicules the vision Macbeth had before he killed Duncan

flaws bursts of passion

starts sudden movements

Impostors false imitations

woman's story ... fire Shakespeare associates sad or frightening tales with women and winter

Authorised ... grandam confirmed by her grandmother

charnel-houses vaults in which the bones of the dead are piled up

monuments graves or last resting places of the dead

maws of kites stomachs of birds of prey

unmanned made weak or timid

If ... here proverb: 'as true as you stand there'

Ere humane statute ... weal before compassionate law banished evil from the lawful commonwealth

mortal fatal

crowns tops of heads; also a reference to the kingly crown that Banquo's children will wear

muse marvel or wonder

infirmity weakness

Come ... all Macbeth proposes the toast he promised at the beginning of the scene

MACBETH	Ay, and a bold one, that dare look on that
	Which might appal the devil.
LADY MACBETH	O proper stuff!	60
	This is the very painting of your fear;
	This is the air-drawn dagger which you said
	Led you to Duncan. O, these flaws and starts,
	Impostors to true fear, would well become
	A woman's story at a winter's fire	65
	Authorised by her grandam. Shame itself!
	Why do you make such faces? When all's done
	You look but on a stool.
MACBETH	Prithee, see there! Behold, look, lo! How say you?
	[*To Ghost*] Why, what care I? If thou canst nod, speak too.	70
	If charnel-houses and our graves must send
	Those that we bury back, our monuments
	Shall be the maws of kites.

[Exit Ghost of Banquo]

LADY MACBETH	What, quite unmanned in folly?
MACBETH	If I stand here, I saw him.
LADY MACBETH	Fie, for shame.
MACBETH	Blood hath been shed ere now, i'th'olden time,	75
	Ere humane statute purged the gentle weal;
	Ay, and since too, murders have been performed
	Too terrible for the ear. The time has been
	That when the brains were out, the man would die,
	And there an end. But now they rise again	80
	With twenty mortal murders on their crowns
	And push us from our stools. This is more strange
	Than such a murder is.
LADY MACBETH	My worthy lord,
	Your noble friends do lack you.
MACBETH	I do forget –
	Do not muse at me, my most worthy friends.	85
	I have a strange infirmity which is nothing
	To those that know me. Come, love and health to all,
	Then I'll sit down. Give me some wine; fill full!

Enter Ghost [of Banquo]

I drink to th'general joy o'th'whole table,

Macbeth, his composure recovered, proposes a toast to Banquo and the guests. On seeing the Ghost again, he bursts into violent language, commanding him away. Lady Macbeth orders the Lords to leave.

Characters

A state dinner to remember

The guests are bewildered and the banquet descends into chaos as Macbeth reacts in horror to the presence of the Ghost.

a Describe how the Ghost enters and behaves during Macbeth's violent outbursts (lines 89–107).

b What does Lady Macbeth make of these events? In some productions she starts to drink heavily during the banquet, and becomes increasingly drunk and exhausted by the end of the scene. Other productions show her directing operations and holding everything together throughout a disastrous dinner. How would you convey the stress she might feel as a result of Duncan's murder and Macbeth's strange behaviour?

c Step into role as Lady Macbeth and imagine what she would write in her secret diary at the end of this scene. Describe what she saw and did at the banquet. How does this make her feel and what is she thinking now?

him we thirst Banquo, for whom we long

duties respects

pledge toast

marrowless lacking life and vitality

speculation sight

peers lords, thanes

Hyrcan tiger savage tiger (supposed to live in Hyrcania, near the Caspian Sea)

Take ... that take any form but that of Banquo's ghost

dare ... desert challenge me (to fight you) in the desert

If trembling ... girl if I tremble, call me the doll or puppet of a girl

admired wondered at, wondrous

overcome pass over or take by surprise

make ... owe make me unlike my usual self

ruby redness

blanched made pale

Question questioning or interrogation

Stand not upon do not be concerned with

order rank or determined protocol

	And to our dear friend Banquo, whom we miss.

And to our dear friend Banquo, whom we miss. 90
Would he were here! To all, and him we thirst,
And all to all.

LORDS   Our duties and the pledge.

MACBETH   Avaunt and quit my sight! Let the earth hide thee!
Thy bones are marrowless, thy blood is cold;
Thou hast no speculation in those eyes 95
Which thou dost glare with.

LADY MACBETH   Think of this, good peers,
But as a thing of custom. 'Tis no other,
Only it spoils the pleasure of the time.

MACBETH   What man dare, I dare;
Approach thou like the rugged Russian bear, 100
The armed rhinoceros, or th'Hyrcan tiger,
Take any shape but that, and my firm nerves
Shall never tremble. Or be alive again,
And dare me to the desert with thy sword;
If trembling I inhabit then, protest me 105
The baby of a girl. Hence horrible shadow,
Unreal mock'ry hence.

[*Exit Ghost of Banquo*]

             Why so, being gone,
I am a man again. – Pray you, sit still.

LADY MACBETH   You have displaced the mirth, broke the good meeting
With most admired disorder.

MACBETH   Can such things be, 110
And overcome us like a summer's cloud,
Without our special wonder? You make me strange
Even to the disposition that I owe,
When now I think you can behold such sights
And keep the natural ruby of your cheeks, 115
When mine is blanched with fear.

ROSS   What sights, my lord?

LADY MACBETH   I pray you speak not; he grows worse and worse.
Question enrages him. At once, good night.
Stand not upon the order of your going,
But go at once.

The Lords leave. Macbeth broods on murder and unnaturalness. He vows to visit the Witches to know his future, swearing that from now on there is no turning back. He will kill anyone standing in his way.

Themes

Evil and blood (by yourself)

After the disturbed action of the banquet, the final episode of the scene is usually played slowly in a still and eerie atmosphere. Macbeth and his wife are left alone together and Macbeth seems to enter a mysterious, personal world of evil and renewed energy.

In role as a psychologist, write an analysis of either Macbeth or Lady Macbeth. Remember to use quotations from the script opposite (especially those that refer to blood as a symbol of guilt or addiction to evil). Refer also to the impact of sleep deprivation and guilt, and the allure of evil for the characters at this point in the play (lines 122–38).

1 'O, full of scorpions' (in tens)

From the first act, Lady Macbeth has influenced her husband by challenging him and manipulating him to murder Duncan and take the throne. During Act 3, we see the impact of the shame that takes hold of Macbeth after he has committed the murder. He tells his wife of his guilt and the strange dreams that haunt him.

Allocate everyone one of the lines below, taken from the play up to this point. Use the following activity to explore Macbeth's mental state at the end of Act 3.

* 'Are you a man?' (Act 3 Scene 4, line 58)
* 'Infirm of purpose!' (Act 2 Scene 2, line 55)
* 'Was the hope drunk / Wherein you dressed yourself?' (Act 1 Scene 7, lines 35–6)
* 'Art thou afeard / To be the same in thine own act and valour, / As thou art in desire?' (Act 1 Scene 7, lines 39–41)
* 'From this time, / Such I account thy love.' (Act 1 Scene 7, lines 38–9)
* 'My hands are of your colour, but I shame / To wear a heart so white.' (Act 2 Scene 2, lines 67–8)
* 'Be not lost / So poorly in your thoughts.' (Act 2 Scene 2, lines 74–5)
* 'This is the very painting of your fear' (Act 3 Scene 4, line 61)
* 'What? Quite unmanned in folly?' (Act 3 Scene 4, line 73)
* 'Shame itself! / Why do you make such faces?' (Act 3 Scene 4, lines 66–7)

Take turns being Macbeth and stand in the middle of the circle as everyone says their lines aggressively, scornfully, insultingly and with force. Feed back to the class your experience of being Macbeth – how did it feel to face such insults and abuse? Afterwards, discuss whether Lady Macbeth's advice to get more sleep is either perfectly acceptable or totally inadequate.

Augures … relations prophecies, and meaningful patterns

maggot-pies, and choughs magpies and a species of crow (birds of ill omen)

secret'st man of blood concealed murderers

What … night? what is the time of night?

at odds with striving with

How sayst thou that what do you think of the fact that

denies his person absents himself

send send a message or messenger

them Scottish nobles

a servant feed a paid spy or bribed servant

will will go

betimes soon, speedily

worst means most evil methods

in head … hand in thought that will become actions

acted … scanned done at once without close thought

initiate inexperienced, first

wants hard use lacks testing or repeated use

young in deed beginners in crime

LENNOX   Good night, and better health   120
              Attend his majesty.

LADY MACBETH   A kind good night to all.
                              [*Exeunt*] *Lords* [*and Attendants*]

MACBETH   It will have blood they say: blood will have blood.
              Stones have been known to move and trees to speak.
              Augures, and understood relations, have
              By maggot-pies, and choughs, and rooks brought forth   125
              The secret'st man of blood. What is the night?

LADY MACBETH   Almost at odds with morning, which is which.

MACBETH   How sayst thou that Macduff denies his person
              At our great bidding?

LADY MACBETH   Did you send to him, sir?

MACBETH   I hear it by the way, but I will send.   130
              There's not a one of them but in his house
              I keep a servant feed. I will tomorrow –
              And betimes I will – to the weïrd sisters.
              More shall they speak. For now I am bent to know
              By the worst means, the worst; for mine own good,   135
              All causes shall give way. I am in blood
              Stepped in so far that should I wade no more,
              Returning were as tedious as go o'er.
              Strange things I have in head that will to hand,
              Which must be acted ere they may be scanned.   140

LADY MACBETH   You lack the season of all natures, sleep.

MACBETH   Come, we'll to sleep. My strange and self-abuse
              Is the initiate fear that wants hard use;
              We are yet but young in deed.

                                              Exeunt

Hecate rebukes the Witches for speaking to Macbeth without involving her. She instructs them to meet her at the pit of Acheron to tell Macbeth of his destiny. She promises to use magic to ruin the over-confident Macbeth.

1 Is it by Shakespeare? (in pairs)

Scene 5 links the previous scene, in which Macbeth decides to visit the Witches, with the opening of Act 4, when he meets them. But there have been many arguments about whether Shakespeare himself wrote the scene. It is generally accepted that another playwright, Thomas Middleton, wrote this scene, as well as some of the Witches' songs in Act 4. The scene opposite has a different rhythmic quality from the rest of the play. It also includes an extra witch, who vanishes dramatically. (The 'foggy cloud' in line 35 may have allowed Hecate a spectacular flying exit.)

In role as director, discuss with a partner (your producer) the reasons for including this scene in a production at your school. Think about how you would cut it down a little, then type out the edited speech with instructions for your actors.

2 Find the lines

Identify the sections in lines 2–35 that match the following parts of Hecate's meaning:

- reasons for anger
- self-centred Macbeth
- meet tomorrow with spells
- I'm off to collect moon-vapour for magic to ruin Macbeth
- Macbeth's future
- my spirit calls.

Language in the play
Trochaic and iambic rhythm (in pairs)

Earlier in the play, the Witches' lines had a distinct **trochaic** rhythm:

> *Fair is foul and foul is fair,*
> *Hover through the fog and filthy air.*

In this scene, Hecate's lines have an **iambic** rhythm:

> *And I the mistress of your charms,*
> *The close contriver of all harms,*

Can you hear the difference between the rhythms in these lines? Describe in your own words the difference between trochaic and iambic rhythm (see 'Verse and prose', p. 172). How is this scene as a whole different to the previous scenes that the Witches appear in? Research these rhythms further by finding extracts from other famous texts and describing the impact of the rhythm in each example.

angerly angry, angrily
beldams hags, witches
Saucy ill-behaved, impudent
traffic trade with or be concerned with

close contriver secret maker

wayward wilful, stubborn

Loves ... ends cares about magic and prophecies for his own purposes
pit sunken place
Acheron river in the classical Hades (hell)

spend use, employ
dismal malign, sinister
fatal destined or destructive
business work

vap'rous drop magical potion

sleights tricks
artificial sprites false spirits
illusion deception

spurn reject contemptuously
bear ... wisdom cherish his hopes more than wisdom or prudence
security over-confidence

Act 3 Scene 5
A desolate place

Thunder. Enter the three WITCHES, *meeting* HECATE

FIRST WITCH Why how now, Hecate, you look angerly?
HECATE Have I not reason, beldams, as you are,
Saucy and over-bold? How did you dare
To trade and traffic with Macbeth
In riddles and affairs of death?   5
And I the mistress of your charms,
The close contriver of all harms,
Was never called to bear my part
Or show the glory of our art?
And which is worse, all you have done   10
Hath been but for a wayward son,
Spiteful and wrathful, who, as others do,
Loves for his own ends, not for you.
But make amends now. Get you gone,
And at the pit of Acheron   15
Meet me i'th'morning. Thither he
Will come to know his destiny.
Your vessels and your spells provide,
Your charms and every thing beside.
I am for th'air. This night I'll spend   20
Unto a dismal and a fatal end.
Great business must be wrought ere noon.
Upon the corner of the moon
There hangs a vap'rous drop profound;
I'll catch it ere it come to ground;   25
And that distilled by magic sleights,
Shall raise such artificial sprites
As by the strength of their illusion
Shall draw him on to his confusion.
He shall spurn fate, scorn death, and bear   30
His hopes 'bove wisdom, grace, and fear.
And you all know, security
Is mortals' chiefest enemy.

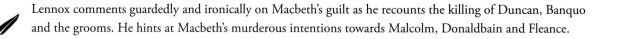

Lennox comments guardedly and ironically on Macbeth's guilt as he recounts the killing of Duncan, Banquo and the grooms. He hints at Macbeth's murderous intentions towards Malcolm, Donaldbain and Fleance.

1 Tyranny and dictatorship (in pairs)

Under a dictatorship, everyone must watch their language. It is dangerous to voice your thoughts openly. Even though the script opposite is more like a monologue than a dialogue, it marks a turning point as the formerly frightened Scots begin to speak out.

Turn Lennox's lines 1–24 into a conversation by speaking small sections in turn and experimenting with using:

- hushed voices
- fearful gestures
- a guarded and suspicious manner
- long, pregnant pauses
- monosyllables for emphasis or double meaning (see line 7)
- marked statement of 'official' perspectives (see line 6)
- insinuating or suggestive gestures.

How would you advise an actor to speak Lennox's lines to show he is on his guard and afraid to speak the truth plainly? What actions might Lennox and his listener use to express this?

2 Dramatic grammar (by yourself)

Read Lennox's lines opposite by yourself as you walk around the room. Pay particular attention to the grammar by changing direction as you walk:

- At each full stop make a full 'about-turn' (180 degrees).
- At each comma make a half turn (90 degrees to your right or left).
- Think of a gesture to make at every question mark (such as stamping your foot or clicking your fingers).

Think about your feelings as you enhance the words with these actions. How might the grammatical structure of the script reflect the character's feelings and experiences?

Write about it

Living under the rule of a murderer

Write a journalist's report describing what life is like for the people of Scotland under the rule of a murderous king. Why does Shakespeare want to provide this perspective on Macbeth's rule?

but hit your thoughts echoed your own beliefs

only I say I only say

strangely borne oddly carried out

pitied of lamented by

marry indeed (by St Mary)

right-valiant very valiant

too late at night

want the thought fail to think

fact deed, action

pious loyal, dutiful

thralls prisoners or slaves

under his key within his power or locked up

an't if it

peace hush, be silent

broad words frank talk

bestows himself lives now

Music, and a song[, 'Come away, come away', within]
Hark, I am called: my little spirit, see,
Sits in a foggy cloud, and stays for me.   [*Exit*]   35
FIRST WITCH Come, let's make haste; she'll soon be back again.

                                              Exeunt

Act 3 Scene 6
The castle of Lennox

Enter LENNOX *and another* LORD

LENNOX My former speeches have but hit your thoughts
Which can interpret further; only I say
Things have been strangely borne. The gracious Duncan
Was pitied of Macbeth; marry, he was dead.
And the right-valiant Banquo walked too late,   5
Whom you may say, if't please you, Fleance killed,
For Fleance fled. Men must not walk too late.
Who cannot want the thought how monstrous
It was for Malcolm and for Donaldbain
To kill their gracious father? Damnèd fact,   10
How it did grieve Macbeth! Did he not straight
In pious rage the two delinquents tear,
That were the slaves of drink and thralls of sleep?
Was not that nobly done? Ay, and wisely too,
For 'twould have angered any heart alive   15
To hear the men deny't. So that I say,
He has borne all things well, and I do think
That had he Duncan's sons under his key –
As, an't please heaven, he shall not – they should find
What 'twere to kill a father. So should Fleance.   20
But peace, for from broad words, and 'cause he failed
His presence at the tyrant's feast, I hear
Macduff lives in disgrace. Sir, can you tell
Where he bestows himself?

93

The unnamed Lord tells of Malcolm's warm welcome in England, and of Macduff's plea to King Edward for an army to overthrow Macbeth's tyranny. He reports Macduff's refusal to visit Macbeth.

1 Who is the unnamed Lord? (in small groups)

The unnamed Lord has a similar dramatic function to the Old Man of Act 2 Scene 4, who represented the ordinary people of Scotland. In this scene, the Lord has words of hope for the eventual peace and prosperity of Scotland.

Identify some of these positive words in lines 24–39. Prepare a tableau contrasting the characters of the Old Man and the unnamed Lord, thinking in terms of 'present Scotland' and 'future Scotland' (for example, starving in the present versus feasting in the future, sleeplessness versus tranquil sleep).

2 'The cloudy messenger' (in pairs)

In several of Shakespeare's plays, the messenger that brings bad news gets into trouble merely for reporting it. Macbeth's 'cloudy messenger' of lines 41–4 is obviously resentful of Macduff's refusal to return to Scotland. It will hinder ('clog') the messenger's career prospects.

Imagine what the messenger travelling back to Macbeth with the bad news of Macduff's answer might say. With a partner, compose the script for the scene in which he tells Macbeth the truth, while hoping to avoid punishment. Experiment with ways of performing your script.

Themes
Internal violence (by yourself)

In Act 1 Scene 2, there are vivid images of violence from the battles fought by the rulers of Scotland to defend the country from Norwegian enemies. In this scene, however, there is evidence of violence and tyranny unleashed against the citizens of Scotland as a result of the evil that has invaded the country through Macbeth's behaviour. Create a table or a Venn diagram that compares the imagery, language and distress of Scotland in these scenes. For example, in Act 1 Scene 2, the battle is described with reference to 'two spent swimmers that do cling together / And choke their art', while in Act 3 Scene 6, Scotland is described as 'suffering country / Under a hand accursed'.

---

son of Duncan Malcolm

holds the due of birth steals his birthright, the crown

Edward King Edward the Confessor (reigned 1042–66)

with such grace ... respect with full dignity, despite the loss of his throne

pray request

him above God

ratify justify

Do ... homage give faithful allegiance

pine yearn or long

this report Malcolm's account of events in Scotland

their king King Edward

attempt of war attack, assault

absolute positive or decided

'Sir, not I' these are Macduff's words

cloudy sullen, frowning

hums murmurs discontentedly

rue the time regret the occasion

clogs burdens or hampers

to a caution to be careful

LORD   The son of Duncan,
From whom this tyrant holds the due of birth,   25
Lives in the English court and is received
Of the most pious Edward with such grace,
That the malevolence of fortune nothing
Takes from his high respect. Thither Macduff
Is gone to pray the holy king upon his aid   30
To wake Northumberland and warlike Siward,
That by the help of these, with him above
To ratify the work, we may again
Give to our tables meat, sleep to our nights,
Free from our feasts and banquets bloody knives,   35
Do faithful homage and receive free honours,
All which we pine for now. And this report
Hath so exasperate their king that he
Prepares for some attempt of war.

LENNOX   Sent he to Macduff?   40

LORD   He did. And with an absolute, 'Sir, not I',
The cloudy messenger turns me his back
And hums, as who should say, 'You'll rue the time
That clogs me with this answer.'

LENNOX   And that well might
Advise him to a caution t'hold what distance   45
His wisdom can provide. Some holy angel
Fly to the court of England and unfold
His message ere he come, that a swift blessing
May soon return to this our suffering country
Under a hand accursed.

LORD   I'll send my prayers with him.   50

                                Exeunt

Looking back at Act 3
Activities for groups or individuals

1 Silent witnesses

Act 3 opens shortly after Macbeth has been crowned at Scone as High King of Scotland, and it includes the dramatic invasion of a stately banquet by the Ghost of Banquo. Step into role as a thane at either event. Invent your thane's title and write *either* an account of the unstaged coronation as seen by a participant *or* an account of the banquet as the thanes are abruptly dismissed in Scene 4. You might like to write this account in your journal or in a letter to a trusted friend.

2 Thematic focus

Look back at the Themes boxes on the left-hand pages, then create a mind map of the themes that have been developed in Act 3. Draw a chart to show how they relate to each other, and support your chart with quotations from the play. Remember that the following themes are interrelated in the play: the relationship between appearance and reality; the manifestation of evil, and honour and loyalty; how selfishness and ambition sit with kingship and honour.

Now present a case to the rest of the class: which are the most important combinations of themes? Why? How have the events of this act contributed to your understanding of them?

3 'Good things of day begin to droop and drowse'

One critic thought that line 52 in Scene 2 was 'the motto of the entire tragedy'. Look through this act in pairs to find other lines that might similarly capture the essence of *Macbeth*, or lines that might work as a subtitle to the play. Write out the lines and explain to other pairs why you think they are significant.

4 Changing relationships

Act 3 is the last time the Macbeths appear together, and we see how their relationship has changed since the beginning of the play. The following activity will help you compare their relationship at the end of Act 1 with their relationship at the end of Act 3.

Create a line diagram to show the changing relationship between this couple. Along the horizontal axis, mark out Act 1, Act 2 and Act 3. Along the vertical axis, mark out the level of power and control the character has, both personally and within the relationship. The highest level shows them to be controlling and manipulative, while the lowest level shows them to be out of control and unsure of what is happening in the relationship. Your line graph should reveal at a glance how the Macbeths' relationship has changed throughout the play so far.

5 The Macbeths psychoanalysed

In role as a psychoanalyst, use your line graph to report on the differences in the Macbeths' states of mind and relationship. You may also want to consider:

- how they speak to each other
- how they talk about the future
- the language and imagery they use
- their ideas of 'manhood' and 'womanhood'
- their mental suffering and anxiety.

Write at least two paragraphs, and remember to identify quotations from the play that would give your report more detail. Finish with an additional paragraph predicting what will happen to the Macbeths in the final two acts of the play.

97

The Witches' familiars have declared the time has come to meet Macbeth. Engrossed in their ugly ritual, they chant as they circle the cauldron, throwing in repulsive ingredients to make a sickening brew.

Stagecraft

What is happening on stage? (in pairs)

The script opposite has a pattern to it: each Witch is given a long speech, and in between they chant a rhyming couplet together. What might each Witch be doing on stage while delivering these lines? With a partner, write detailed stage directions for ten lines from this section. Consider the context and setting for your production to help you work out the characters' movements.

Language in the play

The Witches' words (by yourself)

Shakespeare uses lists that accumulate words or phrases to increase dramatic effect and add to the sinister atmosphere. In a few paragraphs written for a younger student, describe some of the patterns in the language used by the Witches in the script opposite. Identify features of rhyme, rhythm and language such as **assonance** and **alliteration**. (See 'The language of *Macbeth*', pp. 170–3.)

1 Hyphenated adjectives (in pairs)

Find some examples of Shakespeare's hyphenated adjectives in the script opposite. Here are other examples from later in Act 4: 'gold-bound brow'; 'two-fold balls'; 'blood-boltered Banquo'.

a How does this use of language convey striking images or add depth of description to what the Witches are saying? What rhythms or repetitions of sound do they create?

b Write your own hyphenated adjectives as you invent a recipe for either a divine stew, with pleasant ingredients, or another 'hell-broth' with disgusting ingredients.

brindled streaked with colour

hedge-pig hedgehog

Harpier name of a familiar (a harpy had a woman's face and a bird's body); lines 1–3 are about the Witches' familiars (see p. 2)

Sweltered venom poisonous sweat

fenny slimy

fork split tongue

blind-worm slow-worm

howlet young owl

charm magical rhyme

mummy mummified corpse

maw and gulf stomach and throat

ravined full of devoured prey

hemlock poisonous plant

Jew … Turk … Tartar all non-Christians

yew poisonous tree

drab prostitute

slab sticky

chawdron entrails, stomach

98

Act 4 Scene 1
A desolate place near Forres

Thunder. Enter the three WITCHES [*with a cauldron*]

FIRST WITCH Thrice the brindled cat hath mewed.

SECOND WITCH Thrice and once the hedge-pig whined.

THIRD WITCH Harpier cries, ''Tis time, 'tis time.'

FIRST WITCH Round about the cauldron go;
In the poisoned entrails throw. 5
Toad, that under cold stone
Days and nights has thirty-one
Sweltered venom sleeping got,
Boil thou first i'th'charmèd pot.

ALL Double, double toil and trouble; 10
Fire burn, and cauldron bubble.

SECOND WITCH Fillet of a fenny snake,
In the cauldron boil and bake:
Eye of newt, and toe of frog,
Wool of bat, and tongue of dog, 15
Adder's fork, and blind-worm's sting,
Lizard's leg, and howlet's wing,
For a charm of powerful trouble,
Like a hell-broth, boil and bubble.

ALL Double, double toil and trouble, 20
Fire burn, and cauldron bubble.

THIRD WITCH Scale of dragon, tooth of wolf,
Witches' mummy, maw and gulf
Of the ravined salt-sea shark,
Root of hemlock, digged i'th'dark; 25
Liver of blaspheming Jew,
Gall of goat, and slips of yew,
Slivered in the moon's eclipse;
Nose of Turk, and Tartar's lips,
Finger of birth-strangled babe, 30
Ditch-delivered by a drab,
Make the gruel thick and slab.
Add thereto a tiger's chawdron
For th'ingredience of our cauldron.

The Witches complete the preparation of their hellish brew and are congratulated by Hecate. Macbeth enters and challenges them to answer what he asks, irrespective of the most appalling consequences.

1 Tell me – though destruction follows
(in small groups)

Macbeth is obsessed with one thought: the desire to know the future. He appeals to the Witches to answer him, even if the result is the destruction of the world. His language is like that of the Witches: 'I conjure you' is the beginning of a spell or incantation. Using lines 49–60, try one or more of the following activities:

a One person whispers the lines; the others echo every 'though' for emphasis.

b Experiment with changing the order of words in the list. How would you order it? Do you think that the order Shakespeare chose was the most powerful and dramatic?

c One person reads the lines and the others request clarification from the speaker at the end of each line or phrase (use questions that start with 'what', 'why', 'when', 'where'). The speaker then repeats the line or phrase, emphasising the important parts of the speech.

Themes
Images of chaos (in pairs)

a List some of the verbal images of chaos that appear in this section of the script, then talk with a partner about how this disorder relates to Macbeth's evil and selfish ambition.

b Collect photographs or pictures from magazines that might represent the chaos evident in the script opposite. Annotate each picture with relevant quotations.

c What can you decipher (or discover through research) about beliefs in Shakespeare's day about personal disorder and cosmic chaos?

Language in the play
Shared lines (in fours)

Macbeth has 545 part-lines that are shared between characters. Find examples of shared lines in the script opposite. In your groups, read these out without breaking the rhythm of the line. What effect do the shared lines have in this part of the scene, and in the play as a whole?

pricking tingling

black deadly

conjure call on solemnly or in the name of something sacred

yeasty frothy
Confound defeat utterly or overthrow
navigation shipping
bladed ... lodged refers to a superstitious belief that witches had the power to move corn from place to place or to flatten it into 'corn circles' (intricate shapes)
warders owners, keepers
slope bend
nature's germen the seeds of all life

masters helpers of magicians

ALL	Double, double toil and trouble,	35
	Fire burn, and cauldron bubble.	
SECOND WITCH	Cool it with a baboon's blood,	
	Then the charm is firm and good.	

Enter HECATE, *and the other three Witches*

HECATE	O well done! I commend your pains,	
	And every one shall share i'th'gains;	40
	And now about the cauldron sing	
	Like elves and fairies in a ring,	
	Enchanting all that you put in.	

Music, and a song, 'Black spirits, etc.'
[*Exeunt Hecate and the other three Witches*]

SECOND WITCH	By the pricking of my thumbs,	
	Something wicked this way comes;	45
	Open locks, whoever knocks.	

Enter MACBETH

MACBETH	How now, you secret, black, and midnight hags!	
	What is't you do?	
ALL THE WITCHES	A deed without a name.	
MACBETH	I conjure you by that which you profess,	
	Howe'er you come to know it, answer me.	50
	Though you untie the winds and let them fight	
	Against the churches, though the yeasty waves	
	Confound and swallow navigation up,	
	Though bladed corn be lodged and trees blown down,	
	Though castles topple on their warders' heads,	55
	Though palaces and pyramids do slope	
	Their heads to their foundations, though the treasure	
	Of nature's germen tumble altogether	
	Even till destruction sicken: answer me	
	To what I ask you.	
FIRST WITCH	Speak.	
SECOND WITCH	Demand.	
THIRD WITCH	We'll answer.	60
FIRST WITCH	Say, if thou'dst rather hear it from our mouths,	
	Or from our masters'?	
MACBETH	Call 'em, let me see 'em.	

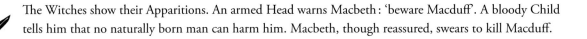

The Witches show their Apparitions. An armed Head warns Macbeth: 'beware Macduff'. A bloody Child tells him that no naturally born man can harm him. Macbeth, though reassured, swears to kill Macduff.

1 Prophetic apparitions (by yourself)

In a table like the one below, briefly describe the three Apparitions, their warnings and what each might symbolise.

Apparition	Warning	Symbolism

Themes

Disorder and evil (in small groups)

a Design *either* a puppet for use on stage to represent one of the Apparitions, *or* an object that one of the Apparitions would hold. You might find inspiration for this from the striking visual and dramatic language in this part of the play. Look for images of dismembered limbs, armour, blood and children. You may also like to refer to objects and images that have a modern (and scary) resonance.

b In your groups, *either* stage the scene as an animation or puppet show, *or* work out a note from a director to his set designer describing how you would like to see the scene staged in the scariest way possible.

Language in the play

Hendiadys (in pairs)

Upon seeing the Third Apparition, Macbeth describes the crown on the child's head as 'the round / And top of sovereignty' (lines 87–8). Shakespeare uses two nouns, instead of an adjective and a noun (round top or rounded top), to describe what Macbeth sees. This is known as a **hendiadys** and it carries more layers of meaning than just saying 'crown'. What different meanings do the words 'round' and 'top' carry in this hendiadys?

Try out your own creative ideas to imitate Shakespeare's device and make up your own hendiadys from these adjective and noun pairs: furious sound; angelic ministers of grace; thankful payment; widely universal theatre; bodily beauty; heavenly grace.

farrow litter of piglets

the murderer's gibbet
where a murderer was hanged

office function, purpose
deftly skilfully

Thane of Fife Macduff
caution word of warning
harped echoed or guessed

potent powerful

assurance double sure
my security even more certain
take a bond of fate
swear a binding oath

issue descendant, child
round … sovereignty the crown

FIRST WITCH	Pour in sow's blood, that hath eaten
	Her nine farrow; grease that's sweaten
	From the murderer's gibbet throw	65
	Into the flame.
ALL THE WITCHES	Come high or low:
	Thyself and office deftly show.

Thunder. [*Enter*] FIRST APPARITION, *an armed Head*

MACBETH	Tell me, thou unknown power –
FIRST WITCH	He knows thy thought;
	Hear his speech, but say thou nought.
FIRST APPARITION	Macbeth, Macbeth, Macbeth: beware Macduff,	70
	Beware the Thane of Fife. Dismiss me. Enough.	*Descends*
MACBETH	Whate'er thou art, for thy good caution, thanks;
	Thou hast harped my fear aright. But one word more –
FIRST WITCH	He will not be commanded. Here's another,
	More potent than the first.	75

Thunder. [*Enter*] SECOND APPARITION, *a bloody Child*

SECOND APPARITION	Macbeth, Macbeth, Macbeth.
MACBETH	Had I three ears, I'd hear thee.
SECOND APPARITION	Be bloody, bold, and resolute; laugh to scorn
	The power of man, for none of woman born
	Shall harm Macbeth.	*Descends*	80
MACBETH	Then live, Macduff, what need I fear of thee?
	But yet I'll make assurance double sure
	And take a bond of fate: thou shalt not live,
	That I may tell pale-hearted fear it lies,
	And sleep in spite of thunder.

Thunder. [*Enter*] THIRD APPARITION, *a Child crowned, with a tree
in his hand*

	What is this,	85
	That rises like the issue of a king
	And wears upon his baby-brow the round
	And top of sovereignty?
ALL THE WITCHES	Listen, but speak not to't.

Stagecraft

A show of eight kings (in small groups)

Many people believe that Shakespeare had King James I very much in mind as he wrote *Macbeth* (see 'The contexts of *Macbeth*', pp. 162–3). The eight kings are supposed to represent the ancestors of James (represented in the photograph below as eight babies delivered by the Witches). King James saw the play shortly after it was written. One story is that the eighth king carried a mirror ('glass') and, at lines 118–19, focused it on the watching King James, who therefore saw his own reflection and heard the promise that his descendants ('many more') would rule England. Read lines 99–123, then in groups:

a Talk about how you would stage the appearances of the eight kings and Banquo's ghost.

b Create a suitable action or gesture for the actors at key points in the script.

c Describe the props you would like the actors to have. For example, perhaps you would like a blindfold for Macbeth to wear, to make it seem like he was hallucinating.

d Consider the soundtrack or sound effects that would increase dramatic tension.

lion-mettled courageous
Who chafes ... conspirers rebels, dissidents

impress force to join an army
Sweet bodements attractive prophecies
high-placed high-ranking
the lease of nature the length of natural life
mortal custom usual life-span

I will be satisfied I must have an answer

sinks probably through a trapdoor in the stage (while the hautboys conceal the sound of the trapdoor)

glass magic crystal showing visions of the future

sear burn
gold-bound brow head surrounded by a crown
Start jump from your sockets
th'crack of doom doomsday, the thunder of the Day of Judgement
two-fold balls representing the two orbs Macbeth carried at his two coronations in Scotland and England
treble sceptres representing the three kingdoms Macbeth now ruled: Scotland, England and Ireland.
blood-boltered spattered in blood
points ... his indicates that they are his descendants

THIRD APPARITION   Be lion-mettled, proud, and take no care
Who chafes, who frets, or where conspirers are.   90
Macbeth shall never vanquished be until
Great Birnam Wood to high Dunsinane hill
Shall come against him.   *Descends*

MACBETH   That will never be:
Who can impress the forest, bid the tree
Unfix his earthbound root? Sweet bodements, good.   95
Rebellious dead, rise never till the wood
Of Birnam rise, and our high-placed Macbeth
Shall live the lease of nature, pay his breath
To time and mortal custom. Yet my heart
Throbs to know one thing. Tell me, if your art   100
Can tell so much, shall Banquo's issue ever
Reign in this kingdom?

ALL THE WITCHES   Seek to know no more.

MACBETH   I will be satisfied. Deny me this,
And an eternal curse fall on you. Let me know.
        [Cauldron descends.] Hautboys
Why sinks that cauldron? And what noise is this?   105

FIRST WITCH   Show!

SECOND WITCH   Show!

THIRD WITCH   Show!

ALL THE WITCHES   Show his eyes and grieve his heart,
Come like shadows, so depart.   110

[Enter] a show of eight kings, and [the] last with a glass in his hand[;
Banquo's Ghost following]

MACBETH   Thou art too like the spirit of Banquo. Down!
Thy crown does sear mine eyeballs. And thy hair,
Thou other gold-bound brow, is like the first;
A third, is like the former. – Filthy hags,
Why do you show me this? – A fourth? Start, eyes!   115
What, will the line stretch out to th'crack of doom?
Another yet? A seventh? I'll see no more.
And yet the eighth appears, who bears a glass
Which shows me many more. And some I see,
That two-fold balls and treble sceptres carry.   120
Horrible sight! Now I see 'tis true,
For the blood-boltered Banquo smiles upon me,
And points at them for his.
        [Exeunt show of kings and Banquo's Ghost]
        What, is this so?

Having presented Banquo's descendants as kings, the Witches dance, then vanish, to Macbeth's anger. Hearing of Macduff's flight, Macbeth resolves to kill every member of Macduff's family he can catch.

1 Getting the Witches off the stage (in small groups)

Lines 124–31 are thought to have been written by Thomas Middleton, and are often cut in production. But many critics argue that the final two lines (130–1) represent another example of Shakespeare flattering King James, and were probably spoken directly to him at a performance in 1606. Whether or not that is true, every new production faces the practical problem of how the Witches leave the stage.

Rewrite the stage direction after line 131 to give more information for actors in a modern production. In your stage direction, include a suitable dance sequence ('antic round', line 129) for the Witches that enables them to 'vanish' as dramatically as possible. Experiment with ways of performing the lines as you think about this.

2 'dread exploits' (in pairs)

The depth of brutality to which Macbeth has now sunk is revealed in his determination to massacre innocent women and children in Macduff's castle. In pairs, take turns to try out different ways of speaking lines 143–54 as:

- private, whispered thoughts
- the words of a very fearful man
- the words of an angry tyrant.

Afterwards, take turns to position your partner into a statue representing the different ways Macbeth could deliver the speech.

Themes

Battling with Time (by yourself)

In his soliloquy, Macbeth expresses a great sense of urgency, as if he is in a battle with Time. He decides that intentions without action are useless, and resolves simply to follow his first instincts without time for second thoughts or the objections of his conscience.

Write a paragraph, using embedded quotations, to consider other references to time in the play so far, and to describe how this theme is developed in the script opposite.

---

amazedly as in a maze

sprites spirits

antic round mad dance

did his welcome pay showed him the respect due to a monarch

aye accursèd cursed for ever

dread terrible or fearsome

flighty purpose quick thoughts, first intentions

never is o'ertook never happens

The very firstlings ... hand I'll act on my first instincts

thought and done like the proverb 'no sooner said than done'

give ... o'th'sword kill

trace him in his line descend from him

FIRST WITCH	Ay, sir, all this is so. But why
	Stands Macbeth thus amazedly? 125
	Come, sisters, cheer we up his sprites,
	And show the best of our delights.
	I'll charm the air to give a sound,
	While you perform your antic round
	That this great king may kindly say, 130
	Our duties did his welcome pay.

Music. The Witches dance, and vanish

MACBETH	Where are they? Gone? Let this pernicious hour,
	Stand aye accursèd in the calendar.
	Come in, without there!

Enter LENNOX

LENNOX	What's your grace's will?
MACBETH	Saw you the weïrd sisters?
LENNOX	No, my lord. 135
MACBETH	Came they not by you?
LENNOX	No indeed, my lord.
MACBETH	Infected be the air whereon they ride,
	And damned all those that trust them. I did hear
	The galloping of horse. Who was't came by?
LENNOX	'Tis two or three, my lord, that bring you word 140
	Macduff is fled to England.
MACBETH	Fled to England?
LENNOX	Ay, my good lord.
MACBETH	[*Aside*] Time, thou anticipat'st my dread exploits;
	The flighty purpose never is o'ertook
	Unless the deed go with it. From this moment, 145
	The very firstlings of my heart shall be
	The firstlings of my hand. And even now
	To crown my thoughts with acts, be it thought and done.
	The castle of Macduff I will surprise;
	Seize upon Fife; give to th'edge o'th'sword 150
	His wife, his babes, and all unfortunate souls
	That trace him in his line. No boasting like a fool;
	This deed I'll do before this purpose cool,
	But no more sights. – Where are these gentlemen?
	Come, bring me where they are. 155

Exeunt

Macduff's wife interprets his flight to England as madness, fear, or lack of love for his family. Ross comforts her: Macduff knows best, and even though the times are dangerous, they will improve.

Write about it

'He loves us not' (by yourself)

Write Lady Macduff's perspective at this point in the play, in the form of a diary entry or a letter to her husband. Does she take comfort from Ross's words and his opinion that evil always gives way to good?

1 Crocodile tears?

In this part of the scene, Ross leaves near to tears. However, in Roman Polanski's 1971 movie, Ross is an obvious hypocrite. As he leaves Macduff's castle, he waves the Murderers in to kill everyone inside, adding to the sense of Scotland's corruption. In other versions, Ross is good-hearted and his words of comfort to Lady Macduff are sincere, but he is naïve in that he underestimates the power of evil against them. Write notes for an actor to explain how you think they should play Ross. Give the actor specific instructions about how to speak and act when playing this scene.

Stagecraft

Scene change (in pairs)

The setting for the action changes from a desolate heath with Witches, bloody Apparitions, rituals and Macbeth's violent thoughts in Scene 1, to Macduff's castle and the innocence of Macduff's wife and child in Scene 2. How would you perform the scene change and set the scene to heighten this contrast? Make two sketches of the designs you would use for the contrasting scenes.

▲ What style of sets would you choose for a production of *Macbeth*? Traditional or modern? Sparse or elaborate?

titles possessions

wants the natural touch lacks feeling for his family

diminutive tiny

All is the fear ... love he's filled with fear, not love

coz cousin

school control

The fits o'th'season the violence of the times

hold rumour ... fear create rumours out of the things we fear

Each way and none go in many directions but settle on no single direction

cousin Lady Macduff's son

Fathered ... fatherless he has a biological father, but he is absent

my disgrace ... discomfort Ross is afraid he will start to weep and embarrass them both

Act 4 Scene 2
Fife The castle of Macduff

Enter LADY MACDUFF, *her* SON, *and* ROSS

LADY MACDUFF   What had he done, to make him fly the land?

ROSS   You must have patience, madam.

LADY MACDUFF   He had none;
His flight was madness. When our actions do not,
Our fears do make us traitors.

ROSS   You know not
Whether it was his wisdom or his fear.   5

LADY MACDUFF   Wisdom? To leave his wife, to leave his babes,
His mansion, and his titles in a place
From whence himself does fly? He loves us not.
He wants the natural touch, for the poor wren,
The most diminutive of birds, will fight,   10
Her young ones in her nest, against the owl.
All is the fear, and nothing is the love;
As little is the wisdom, where the flight
So runs against all reason.

ROSS   My dearest coz,
I pray you school yourself. But for your husband,   15
He is noble, wise, judicious, and best knows
The fits o'th'season. I dare not speak much further,
But cruel are the times when we are traitors
And do not know ourselves, when we hold rumour
From what we fear, yet know not what we fear,   20
But float upon a wild and violent sea,
Each way and none. I take my leave of you;
Shall not be long but I'll be here again.
Things at the worst will cease, or else climb upward
To what they were before. My pretty cousin,   25
Blessing upon you.

LADY MACDUFF   Fathered he is, and yet he's fatherless.

ROSS   I am so much a fool, should I stay longer
It would be my disgrace and your discomfort.
I take my leave at once.   *Exit*

Macduff's son teases his mother affectionately. Behind his playful words are glimpses of the dangerous times: traps for the innocent and widespread treachery. A messenger arrives to warn of danger.

Themes

A man's duty (whole class)

Macduff has fled to England to raise enough forces to overthrow the increasingly murderous Macbeth. However, in doing so he has left his wife and family behind, and they are now at risk themselves. Lady Macduff tells her son that his father is 'dead' and a 'traitor'. She seems to want to remove him from their lives, perhaps to protect her son. But the boy continues to intelligently question the truth of what she says.

As a class, debate Macduff's actions. Should he have stayed and protected his family (which would mean that perhaps many more would be killed by Macbeth)? Or was he right to act as he did? Ask yourselves: should our first sense of duty be to ourselves, our loved ones or our country?

Characters

The 'mind's construction' (in pairs)

The photograph of Lady Macduff below prompts comparisons with depictions of Lady Macbeth.

a   What are the main differences between these women, specifically in terms of their ideas about children, husband and family?

b   In conversation with your partner, suggest several ways in which this image conveys the innocence and vulnerability that Macbeth is determined to destroy.

Sirrah affectionate use of 'sir'
dead metaphorically dead or absent

lime/pitfall/gin methods of catching birds: a glue-like paste smeared on trees / a pit / a trap to catch a bird by the head or legs
Poor birds ... set for small birds are not in danger of traps (only larger birds had traps set for them)

swears takes an oath, vows to tell the truth

prattler chatterbox

in your state ... perfect I have only good intentions towards you
doubt suspect or fear

LADY MACDUFF   Sirrah, your father's dead,   30
      And what will you do now? How will you live?

SON   As birds do, mother.

LADY MACDUFF   What, with worms and flies?

SON   With what I get I mean, and so do they.

LADY MACDUFF   Poor bird, thou'dst never fear the net, nor lime,
      the pitfall, nor the gin.   35

SON   Why should I, mother? Poor birds they are not set for.
      My father is not dead for all your saying.

LADY MACDUFF   Yes, he is dead. How wilt thou do for a father?

SON   Nay, how will you do for a husband?

LADY MACDUFF   Why, I can buy me twenty at any market.   40

SON   Then you'll buy 'em to sell again.

LADY MACDUFF   Thou speak'st with all thy wit, and yet i'faith
      with wit enough for thee.

SON   Was my father a traitor, mother?

LADY MACDUFF   Ay, that he was.   45

SON   What is a traitor?

LADY MACDUFF   Why, one that swears and lies.

SON   And be all traitors, that do so?

LADY MACDUFF   Every one that does so is a traitor and must be
      hanged.   50

SON   And must they all be hanged that swear and lie?

LADY MACDUFF   Every one.

SON   Who must hang them?

LADY MACDUFF   Why, the honest men.

SON   Then the liars and swearers are fools, for there are liars and   55
      swearers enough to beat the honest men and hang up them.

LADY MACDUFF   Now God help thee, poor monkey, but how wilt
      thou do for a father?

SON   If he were dead, you'd weep for him; if you would not, it were
      a good sign that I should quickly have a new father.   60

LADY MACDUFF   Poor prattler, how thou talk'st!

Enter a MESSENGER

MESSENGER   Bless you, fair dame. I am not to you known,
      Though in your state of honour I am perfect;
      I doubt some danger does approach you nearly.

The messenger warns Lady Macduff to flee with her children because terrible danger is near. The Murderers enter, seeking Macduff. They kill his son and pursue Macduff's wife to murder her off stage.

Themes

Slaughter of the Innocents (in pairs)

One critic compared this scene to the biblical Slaughter of the Innocents. Macbeth's murder of future life and youthful hopefulness, as well as his cruelty and depravity, take on epic proportions through this biblical allusion.

Find pictures of the Slaughter of the Innocents and then look at Lady Macduff's lines 70–4. Why are Macbeth's murderous intentions so disturbing in this part of the play? Use the style and tone of the front page of a tabloid newspaper to report these events.

Stagecraft

On stage or off stage?

In Greek tragedy, all killings took place off stage. The audience did not see the act of violence, but heard it reported later. Shakespeare devotes very few lines to the murders, but productions vary greatly in their presentation, often showing Lady Macduff killed on stage.

How would you stage the final few lines? Should she be killed on or off stage? How would you advise the actor playing Lady Macduff to show her bravery and defiance as she insults the Murderers? How would you portray the son's loyalty to his father and his bravery in the face of death? Write a paragraph giving reasons for your decisions.

1 Murderers most foul (in small groups)

Think about status, gestures and interaction between the characters in this murder scene. Split your group into people of high and low status. Experiment with ways of interacting with each other, following these rules:

- Give high-status characters strong gestures, upright postures, with lifted eyes and movements forward with purpose.
- Give low-status characters insecure gestures, slouching postures, lowered eyes and shuffling movements that have no purpose.

How does this activity give you more insight into the scene and the tragedy that develops?

homely friendly

Hence go away or depart

methinks it seems to me

fell cruelty deadly danger

Which is ... person which is close at hand

laudable praiseworthy

unsanctified unholy

shag-haired long, shaggy hair (the sign of a villain)

egg insulting description of a young person

fry young fish (notice how images of fertility are used as terms of abuse: 'egg' and 'fry')

112

        If you will take a homely man's advice,   65
        Be not found here. Hence with your little ones.
        To fright you thus, methinks I am too savage;
        To do worse to you were fell cruelty,
        Which is too nigh your person. Heaven preserve you,
        I dare abide no longer.   *Exit*

LADY MACDUFF   Whither should I fly?   70
        I have done no harm. But I remember now
        I am in this earthly world where to do harm
        Is often laudable, to do good sometime
        Accounted dangerous folly. Why then, alas,
        Do I put up that womanly defence,   75
        To say I have done no harm?

                Enter MURDERERS

                     What are these faces?

A MURDERER   Where is your husband?

LADY MACDUFF   I hope in no place so unsanctified,
        Where such as thou mayst find him.

A MURDERER   He's a traitor.

SON   Thou liest, thou shag-haired villain.

A MURDERER   What, you egg!   80
        Young fry of treachery!
                [*Kills him*]

SON   He has killed me, mother,
        Run away, I pray you!
        Exit [*Lady Macduff*] *crying 'Murder'*[, *pursued by*
                 Murderers with her Son]

Macduff urges Malcolm to go to the defence of Scotland, which is suffering under Macbeth's tyranny. Malcolm voices his suspicions that Macduff is Macbeth's agent and has good reasons to betray him to Macbeth.

Stagecraft

England: design the scene (in pairs)

Work out a simple but effective way of showing the audience that this scene takes place in England at the palace of King Edward.

desolate shade remote place

1 Malcolm's suspicions about Macduff

(in small groups)

Malcolm builds a strong case for his mistrust of Macduff:

- He is not sure that Macduff is telling the truth (line 11).
- Macbeth was once thought to be honest (lines 12–13).
- Macduff was a friend of Macbeth (line 13).
- Macbeth has left Macduff unharmed (line 14).
- Macduff may betray Malcolm to Macbeth (lines 14–15).
- Macduff may kill Malcolm for Macbeth (lines 16–17).
- Macbeth is a traitor (line 18).
- Even a good man may obey a wicked king (lines 19–20).
- Evil often tries to look like good (lines 21–3).
- Macduff has abruptly left his family behind in danger (lines 26–8).
- Malcolm is suspicious for his own safety (lines 29–30).

Imagine you are Malcolm and draw up a list of questions that you would like to ask Macduff. Afterwards, take turns playing Macduff and answering the questions from the rest of the group.

fast firmly or tightly
mortal fatal or deadly
Bestride ... birthdoms defend our suffering birthplace or inheritance
Like syllable of dolour similar cry of grief

redress make better
to friend as a friend or on my side

discern of be rewarded by

Language in the play

Religious imagery

There is much religious imagery in the speeches opposite, including references to sorrow that strikes heaven on the face (line 6), an innocent lamb (line 16) and to angels and fallen angels (line 22).

Write an extended paragraph describing this imagery to a younger student. How do these images relate to themes of good and evil, deceptive appearances and disorder in the natural world? How can each of them apply to Macbeth himself? To extend your ideas, look through the act to find other examples of religious imagery.

recoil / In an imperial charge serve a royal command
crave beg
transpose change
the brightest Lucifer (who fell from God's grace)
the brows of grace the look of goodness

rawness incompleteness

114

Act 4 Scene 3
England The palace of King Edward

Enter MALCOLM *and* MACDUFF

MALCOLM	Let us seek out some desolate shade and there
	Weep our sad bosoms empty.
MACDUFF	Let us rather

MACDUFF   Let us rather

MALCOLM Let us seek out some desolate shade and there
Weep our sad bosoms empty.

MACDUFF   Let us rather
Hold fast the mortal sword and like good men
Bestride our downfall birthdom; each new morn,
New widows howl, new orphans cry, new sorrows   5
Strike heaven on the face, that it resounds
As if it felt with Scotland and yelled out
Like syllable of dolour.

MALCOLM   What I believe, I'll wail;
What know, believe; and what I can redress,
As I shall find the time to friend, I will.   10
What you have spoke, it may be so perchance.
This tyrant, whose sole name blisters our tongues,
Was once thought honest; you have loved him well –
He hath not touched you yet. I am young, but something
You may discern of him through me, and wisdom   15
To offer up a weak, poor, innocent lamb
T'appease an angry god.

MACDUFF I am not treacherous.

MALCOLM   But Macbeth is.
A good and virtuous nature may recoil
In an imperial charge. But I shall crave your pardon: 20
That which you are, my thoughts cannot transpose;
Angels are bright still, though the brightest fell.
Though all things foul would wear the brows of grace,
Yet grace must still look so.

MACDUFF   I have lost my hopes.

MALCOLM Perchance even there where I did find my doubts. 25
Why in that rawness left you wife and child,
Those precious motives, those strong knots of love,
Without leave-taking? I pray you,

Characters

Inner thoughts (in fours)

Malcolm is testing Macduff's sincerity. The terror of Macbeth's regime has made him suspect all visitors – after all, they may be Macbeth's secret agents. He now embarks on a strange way of testing Macduff's honesty, claiming that his own vices far exceed Macbeth's. To explore the complexity of motive and expression in this scene, try the following activity.

Split your group into two pairs. One pair reads the script in role as Malcolm and Macduff. As you read, pause after each speech so that the second pair can voice Malcolm's and Macduff's inner thoughts. If you are in the second pair, try speaking over the shoulder of – or while seated behind – the character whose inner thoughts you are revealing. Talk together about why Malcolm embarks on this bizarre strategy, how effective you think it is going to be and the impact it has on Macduff.

Language in the play

Language and themes

In the script opposite, Shakespeare uses:

*   personification (of Scotland)
*   symbolic language (black, white)
*   religious imagery (hell, devil).

Identify examples of each of these uses of language. How do they relate to the themes of evil, ambition, deception and power that have been developed in the play so far?

jealousies suspicions

lay thou thy basis sure rest secure

check limit or control

affeered confirmed (that is to say, Macbeth is securely king)

to boot as well

absolute total

the yoke slavery

withal besides

hands uplifted in my right soldiers supporting me

England the King of England was Edward the Confessor, known as a holy king

sundry various or diverse

grafted rooted, ingrained

be opened come to flower or be made known

confineless harms limitless evils

legions multitudes or hordes

Let not my jealousies be your dishonours,
But mine own safeties; you may be rightly just,   30
Whatever I shall think.

MACDUFF   Bleed, bleed, poor country.
Great tyranny, lay thou thy basis sure,
For goodness dare not check thee; wear thou thy wrongs,
The title is affeered. Fare thee well, lord,
I would not be the villain that thou think'st   35
For the whole space that's in the tyrant's grasp,
And the rich East to boot.

MALCOLM   Be not offended.
I speak not as in absolute fear of you:
I think our country sinks beneath the yoke;
It weeps, it bleeds, and each new day a gash   40
Is added to her wounds. I think withal
There would be hands uplifted in my right,
And here from gracious England have I offer
Of goodly thousands. But for all this,
When I shall tread upon the tyrant's head,   45
Or wear it on my sword, yet my poor country
Shall have more vices than it had before,
More suffer, and more sundry ways than ever,
By him that shall succeed.

MACDUFF   What should he be?

MALCOLM It is myself I mean – in whom I know   50
All the particulars of vice so grafted
That when they shall be opened, black Macbeth
Will seem as pure as snow, and the poor state
Esteem him as a lamb, being compared
With my confineless harms.

MACDUFF   Not in the legions   55
Of horrid hell can come a devil more damned
In evils to top Macbeth.

Malcolm lists Macbeth's vices, but claims that his own sexual desire is limitless, and he is infinitely greedy. Macduff finds reasons to excuse Malcolm's ungovernable lust and avarice.

Characters

Show Macbeth's evil (in large groups)

Malcolm begins by naming eight of Macbeth's evils. He is 'bloody' (murderous), 'luxurious' (lecherous), 'avaricious' (greedy), 'false', 'deceitful', 'sudden' (violent), 'malicious', and possesses 'every sin / That has a name' (the seven deadly sins). The activity below provides an interesting way to explore the language in lists such as the one in lines 57–60.

Work out a sequence of tableaux or short mimes to show Macbeth's nature. Each scene in your tableaux should show one of the evils listed. Add a commentary to your presentation.

1 Lust and greed: 'portable' sins? (in pairs)

Malcolm claims that he is infinitely lustful and excessively greedy. He says that when he is king, he will satisfy his desire for sex and money. Macduff dismisses these sins as personal flaws that are unimportant as long as a man shows 'other graces', such as the duties owed by a king to his country.

a Do you agree that lust and greed are unimportant in a leader? Does it matter if a ruler is promiscuous or embezzles public money? Talk together about Macduff's reasoning and what it suggests about his character.

b Research and then make a list of real leaders who fit Malcolm's sins. Use examples of the much-publicised sexual and financial activities of modern politicians, as well as leaders of the past.

◀ A historical parallel shows that Malcolm has good reason for his suspicion of visitors. Leon Trotsky was Stalin's friend and ally in the Russian Revolution of 1917, but he later fled Russia to escape Stalin's tyranny. One of Stalin's agents tricked his way into Trotsky's confidence in his safe haven in Mexico, then assassinated him with an ice-pick. Tyrants never forgive or forget.

---

luxurious lustful, lecherous
avaricious greedy or grasping
Sudden rash, violent
smacking having the flavour of
voluptuousness lust
cistern tank
continent impediments restraints

Boundless intemperance limitless lust

hoodwink deceive
there cannot be … so inclined you cannot be so lustful as to take advantage of the many immoral women who might want to be a king's mistress

ill-composed affection wicked emotions
staunchless avarice unstoppable greed

summer-seeming short-lived

foisons harvest or abundance
your mere own simply of your own
portable bearable

MALCOLM   I grant him bloody,
Luxurious, avaricious, false, deceitful,
Sudden, malicious, smacking of every sin
That has a name. But there's no bottom, none,   60
In my voluptuousness: your wives, your daughters,
Your matrons, and your maids could not fill up
The cistern of my lust, and my desire
All continent impediments would o'erbear
That did oppose my will. Better Macbeth,   65
Than such an one to reign.

MACDUFF   Boundless intemperance
In nature is a tyranny; it hath been
Th'untimely emptying of the happy throne
And fall of many kings. But fear not yet
To take upon you what is yours: you may   70
Convey your pleasures in a spacious plenty
And yet seem cold. The time you may so hoodwink.
We have willing dames enough; there cannot be
That vulture in you to devour so many
As will to greatness dedicate themselves,   75
Finding it so inclined.

MALCOLM   With this, there grows
In my most ill-composed affection such
A stanchless avarice that, were I king,
I should cut off the nobles for their lands,
Desire his jewels, and this other's house,   80
And my more-having would be as a sauce
To make me hunger more, that I should forge
Quarrels unjust against the good and loyal,
Destroying them for wealth.

MACDUFF   This avarice
Sticks deeper, grows with more pernicious root   85
Than summer-seeming lust, and it hath been
The sword of our slain kings; yet do not fear,
Scotland hath foisons to fill up your will
Of your mere own. All these are portable,
With other graces weighed.   90

Malcolm claims that he has no good qualities whatsoever, and seeks only to create chaos. Macduff condemns Malcolm as unfit to rule. Malcolm says that Macduff's reaction has removed his suspicions. He denies all vices.

1 The good king (in small groups)

In lines 92–4, Malcolm lists twelve qualities that a good king should possess: 'justice' (fairness), 'verity' (truthfulness), 'temp'rance' (self-control), 'stableness' (even-temperedness), 'bounty' (generosity), 'perseverance' (endurance), 'mercy' (forgiveness), 'lowliness' (humility), 'devotion' (piety), 'patience', 'courage' and 'fortitude' (strength). Do you agree? List these qualities in the order you think is the most important for a good king. Share your list with other groups in the class to see if there is general agreement or not. Remember to justify your top three qualities.

2 Who's who? (in pairs)

Macduff's impassioned outburst in lines 102–14 includes references to Malcolm, Macbeth, Duncan, Duncan's wife, Scotland and Macduff himself. As one person reads a line at a time, the other identifies aloud to whom (or what) Macduff is referring (for example, in line 102 it is 'Malcolm', in line 103, 'Malcolm' and 'Scotland').

Language in the play
Visual images of chaos and uproar

Macduff can tolerate no more of Malcolm's self-condemnation, and rejects him as unfit to live. Look at lines 97–100 and draw an image prompted by the language. How do the images here relate to other visual images in the play based on milk, hell and uproar?

▼ How can costumes reveal what qualities a character possesses?

division variety
several individual
concord peace
Uproar throw into confusion

truest issue legitimate heir
interdiction condemnation
blaspheme his breed slander his family
upon her knees praying

scruples suspicions

trains tricks
modest wisdom common sense
over-credulous haste gullible and foolish speed

detraction accusations
abjure reject

For as
forsworn untruthful

120

MALCOLM   But I have none. The king-becoming graces –
             As justice, verity, temp'rance, stableness,
             Bounty, perseverance, mercy, lowliness,
             Devotion, patience, courage, fortitude –
             I have no relish of them, but abound   95
             In the division of each several crime,
             Acting it many ways. Nay, had I power, I should
             Pour the sweet milk of concord into hell,
             Uproar the universal peace, confound
             All unity on earth.

MACDUFF   O Scotland, Scotland!   100

MALCOLM   If such a one be fit to govern, speak.
             I am as I have spoken.

MACDUFF   Fit to govern?
             No, not to live. O nation miserable!
             With an untitled tyrant, bloody-sceptred,
             When shalt thou see thy wholesome days again,   105
             Since that the truest issue of thy throne
             By his own interdiction stands accursed
             And does blaspheme his breed? Thy royal father
             Was a most sainted king; the queen that bore thee,
             Oft'ner upon her knees than on her feet,   110
             Died every day she lived. Fare thee well,
             These evils thou repeat'st upon thyself
             Hath banished me from Scotland. O my breast,
             Thy hope ends here.

MALCOLM   Macduff, this noble passion,
             Child of integrity, hath from my soul   115
             Wiped the black scruples, reconciled my thoughts
             To thy good truth and honour. Devilish Macbeth
             By many of these trains hath sought to win me
             Into his power, and modest wisdom plucks me
             From over-credulous haste; but God above   120
             Deal between thee and me, for even now
             I put myself to thy direction and
             Unspeak mine own detraction, here abjure
             The taints and blames I laid upon myself,
             For strangers to my nature. I am yet   125
             Unknown to woman, never was forsworn,

Malcolm asserts his virtue and declares he is now ready to invade Scotland. The Doctor tells how King Edward cures sick people by his touch. Malcolm says the gift of healing is passed down to future kings.

1 'Why are you silent?' (in small groups)

Macduff's outburst finally convinces Malcolm that Macduff is sincere. In response, Malcolm reveals his true nature (lines 125–31) and confesses that he has been testing him. How does Macduff react (see line 137)? Some productions make Macduff's disorientation a comic moment; others imply that Macduff might now feel unsure about his alliance with Malcolm.

Take turns as Macduff and answer questions from the rest of the group about his thoughts, feelings, hopes and fears at this point in the play. Then write an aside to insert into the scene, so that an audience will have a greater understanding of Macduff's character and motivations.

Characters

Dramatic contrast (by yourself)

The Doctor's description highlights a contrast between the two kings: Macbeth is dedicated to destruction, King Edward to healing. Where Macbeth unleashes violence and death in his kingdom, King Edward is concerned for his nation's moral and spiritual health.

Identify the images of saintliness found in the description of the ceremony of healing, then compare these with images that have been used to describe Macbeth so far (revisit lines 55–7, 104, 117). Write an obituary for both kings, using these images and your own ideas.

▼ 'This good king'. Imagine that King Edward makes an appearance on stage. How would you have him look, move and speak to set him apart as the 'good king' to Macbeth's 'evil king'?

coveted desired

here-approach arrival here

at a point prepared for war
Now we'll together now we'll journey together
the chance ... quarrel a good outcome be the result of our unfair battle

crew company
stay his cure await his healing touch
their malady ... art their illnesses defeat the efforts of medical science
sanctity holiness
amend are healed
the Evil scrofula, a type of tuberculosis
here-remain stay
solicits entreats
strangely visited very ill people suffering from 'the Evil'
mere very or entire
stamp coin or medal

succeeding royalty the following kings and queens
benediction blessing
With ... virtue in addition to this unusual quality
sundry various
speak proclaim

Scarcely have coveted what was mine own,
At no time broke my faith, would not betray
The devil to his fellow, and delight
No less in truth than life. My first false speaking   130
Was this upon myself. What I am truly
Is thine, and my poor country's, to command:
Whither indeed, before thy here-approach,
Old Siward with ten thousand warlike men
Already at a point was setting forth.   135
Now we'll together, and the chance of goodness
Be like our warranted quarrel. Why are you silent?

MACDUFF   Such welcome and unwelcome things at once,
'Tis hard to reconcile.

Enter a DOCTOR

MALCOLM   Well, more anon. –
Comes the king forth, I pray you?   140

DOCTOR   Ay, sir: there are a crew of wretched souls
That stay his cure; their malady convinces
The great assay of art, but at his touch,
Such sanctity hath heaven given his hand,
They presently amend.   *Exit*   145

MALCOLM   I thank you, doctor.

MACDUFF   What's the disease he means?

MALCOLM   'Tis called the Evil.
A most miraculous work in this good king,
Which often since my here-remain in England   150
I have seen him do. How he solicits heaven
Himself best knows, but strangely visited people
All swoll'n and ulcerous, pitiful to the eye,
The mere despair of surgery, he cures,
Hanging a golden stamp about their necks   155
Put on with holy prayers, and 'tis spoken
To the succeeding royalty he leaves
The healing benediction. With this strange virtue,
He hath a heavenly gift of prophecy,
And sundry blessings hang about his throne   160
That speak him full of grace.

Enter ROSS

MACDUFF   See who comes here.

Themes

'Alas, poor country' (in pairs)

Under Macbeth's rule, Scotland is a country that is 'Almost afraid to know itself' and uncertain of its own identity. Life there has become so full of suffering that 'violent sorrow' is commonplace. Death is so much a fact of everyday experience that good men are more vulnerable than plucked flowers: they do not live as long.

Do you think it is possible for a country to have an identity? Write down words that you would associate with your own country's identity. Use these words to write ten lines of blank verse describing your country and the experiences of specific people living there today.

Language in the play

Key words and images (in pairs)

Read through lines 166–75 slowly. Try to work out an action or gesture for a key word or image in each line. Afterwards, identify some of the language features Shakespeare uses in the script (look for personification, lists, metaphors, visual images, symbols). Record your findings in a table that shows:

- quotations
- language features
- the effect of these language features on an audience or reader.

1 Bringing bad news (in fours)

Ross knows what has happened to Macduff's family. But he does not immediately tell his terrible news, saying rather that they are 'well' and 'at peace'. What different meanings do these key phrases have? Why does Ross delay telling Macduff what has happened? How does this add to the dramatic tension and pathos of the scene?

Read through lines 178–82 in role as Ross, Macduff and Malcolm, with the fourth member of your group acting as an observer. Discuss with the observer your reasons for the pace and tone of each speech, the words to which you gave special emphasis and how you used pauses or gesture for dramatic effect. Using this information, each group's observer reports back to the rest of the class.

---

betimes swiftly
means intervening conditions

once ever
rend tear
not marked go unnoticed
modern ecstasy everyday feeling

or ere before
relation story
nice accurate

doth hiss the speaker is just stale news
teems gives birth to

niggard miser

out in rebellion

power army
afoot marching
eye presence
doff remove

MALCOLM	My countryman, but yet I know him not.
MACDUFF	My ever gentle cousin, welcome hither.
MALCOLM	I know him now. Good God betimes remove
	The means that makes us strangers.
ROSS	Sir, amen. 165
MACDUFF	Stands Scotland where it did?
ROSS	Alas, poor country,
	Almost afraid to know itself. It cannot
	Be called our mother, but our grave, where nothing,
	But who knows nothing, is once seen to smile;
	Where sighs, and groans, and shrieks that rend the air 170
	Are made, not marked; where violent sorrow seems
	A modern ecstasy. The deadman's knell
	Is there scarce asked for who, and good men's lives
	Expire before the flowers in their caps,
	Dying or ere they sicken.
MACDUFF	O relation 175
	Too nice, and yet too true.
MALCOLM	What's the newest grief?
ROSS	That of an hour's age doth hiss the speaker;
	Each minute teems a new one.
MACDUFF	How does my wife?
ROSS	Why, well.
MACDUFF	And all my children?
ROSS	Well, too.
MACDUFF	The tyrant has not battered at their peace? 180
ROSS	No, they were well at peace when I did leave 'em.
MACDUFF	Be not a niggard of your speech: how goes't?
ROSS	When I came hither to transport the tidings
	Which I have heavily borne, there ran a rumour
	Of many worthy fellows that were out, 185
	Which was to my belief witnessed the rather
	For that I saw the tyrant's power afoot.
	Now is the time of help. [*To Malcolm*] Your eye in Scotland
	Would create soldiers, make our women fight
	To doff their dire distresses.
MALCOLM	Be't their comfort 190
	We are coming thither. Gracious England hath
	Lent us good Siward and ten thousand men –

Ross tells of the murder of Macduff's family. Malcolm tries to comfort Macduff, who struggles with his grief over the slaughter of his wife and children.

1 Approach, retreat or manoeuvre (in threes)

Take parts as Ross, Macduff and Malcolm and speak everything from line 195 ('But I have words') to the end of the scene. After you have read it through once, perform it again on your feet, using the following three actions: approach, retreat or manoeuvre. Use these gestures at appropriate times as you read your character's lines. Ask yourselves the following questions as you think about which gestures work best:

- Why might you approach someone or something in everyday life?
- Why might you retreat from something or someone?
- Why might you manoeuvre or reposition yourself in the same space?

Stagecraft

Telling the terrible news

Notice that Ross still delays, then reports bluntly in lines 206–7. What might be happening on stage to make him suddenly break the news like this? Also notice how Macduff presses for detail, then incredulously repeats 'all' four times in lines 218–21, as though he is unable to believe the enormity of what has happened.

How would you advise an actor to use this repetition to greatest dramatic effect? How would you advise him to use pauses and gesture in this scene? Write out your advice and look carefully at any clues for actions (such as in line 210) as you do so.

latch catch

The general cause everyone
fee-grief personal sorrow

heaviest saddest

quarry heap of slaughtered animals

pull your hat upon your brows
a gesture of sorrow or melancholy
o'erfraught overburdened

be from thence be away
from home

hell-kite bird of prey from hell
dam mother
fell swoop fierce or savage attack

An older and a better soldier none
That Christendom gives out.

ROSS   Would I could answer
This comfort with the like. But I have words   195
That would be howled out in the desert air,
Where hearing should not latch them.

MACDUFF   What concern they?
The general cause, or is it a fee-grief
Due to some single breast?

ROSS   No mind that's honest
But in it shares some woe, though the main part   200
Pertains to you alone.

MACDUFF   If it be mine,
Keep it not from me; quickly let me have it.

ROSS   Let not your ears despise my tongue forever
Which shall possess them with the heaviest sound
That ever yet they heard.

MACDUFF   H'm – I guess at it.   205
ROSS   Your castle is surprised; your wife and babes
Savagely slaughtered. To relate the manner
Were on the quarry of these murdered deer
To add the death of you.

MALCOLM   Merciful heaven –
What, man, ne'er pull your hat upon your brows: 210
Give sorrow words; the grief that does not speak,
Whispers the o'erfraught heart and bids it break.

MACDUFF My children too?

ROSS   Wife, children, servants, all
That could be found.

MACDUFF   And I must be from thence?
My wife killed too?

ROSS   I have said.

MALCOLM   Be comforted.   215
Let's make us med'cines of our great revenge
To cure this deadly grief.

MACDUFF He has no children. All my pretty ones?
Did you say all? O hell-kite! All?
What, all my pretty chickens and their dam   220
At one fell swoop?

Macduff cannot hide his grief. He feels that he is to blame for his family's death. He vows vengeance on Macbeth. Malcolm declares that the time is ripe to overthrow Macbeth, as heaven itself is against him.

Write about it

What is a man? (in pairs)

Planning the murder of Duncan, Lady Macbeth taunted Macbeth for not behaving like 'a man', and at the banquet she accused him of being 'unmanned'. Now Malcolm (lines 222 and 238) and Macduff (line 224) express different interpretations of what it is to be a man.

With a partner, talk about whether you agree with their representations of masculinity. Afterwards, write two paragraphs comparing two or more different representations of masculinity in the play so far. Remember to use embedded quotations and to consider how context (the battlefield, domestic sphere, in exile, on the throne) impacts on masculinity.

Characters

Malcolm's motivation (by yourself)

Earlier in the scene, Malcolm had engaged in a deception to test Macduff's integrity. His words now pose a moral question. Is Malcolm genuinely trying to help Macduff cope with his grief, or is he seizing an opportunity to urge him into the common cause against Macbeth? Step into role as Malcolm and write a letter to Donaldbain, currently in self-imposed exile in Ireland, telling him why you behaved as you did throughout this scene.

1 The longest scene (whole class)

Some directors do not include the whole of this scene in their stage productions because it is so long.

a Imagine you are about to put on the play. Split the class in half. One half argues for cutting the scene, the other half for keeping it as it is. Listen carefully to your opponents' reasons to cut or not to cut, and try to answer them.

b Assume you have decided to compromise. You will keep the scene but try to reduce its length. Explore ways of presenting it in the briefest time while still keeping all its major elements.

Naught wicked
demerits faults

whetstone sharpening stone

play … mine eyes weep
braggart boaster
intermission pause in action
Front to front face to face
scape escape
tune mood or manner

Our lack … leave we have only to make our farewells
powers above angels
instruments weapons

MALCOLM	Dispute it like a man.
MACDUFF	I shall do so;
	But I must also feel it as a man;
	I cannot but remember such things were 225
	That were most precious to me. Did heaven look on,
	And would not take their part? Sinful Macduff,
	They were all struck for thee. Naught that I am,
	Not for their own demerits but for mine,
	Fell slaughter on their souls. Heaven rest them now. 230
MALCOLM	Be this the whetstone of your sword, let grief
	Convert to anger. Blunt not the heart, enrage it.
MACDUFF	O, I could play the woman with mine eyes
	And braggart with my tongue. But gentle heavens,
	Cut short all intermission. Front to front 235
	Bring thou this fiend of Scotland and myself;
	Within my sword's length set him. If he scape,
	Heaven forgive him too.
MALCOLM	This tune goes manly.
	Come, go we to the king; our power is ready;
	Our lack is nothing but our leave. Macbeth 240
	Is ripe for shaking, and the powers above
	Put on their instruments. Receive what cheer you may:
	The night is long that never finds the day.

Exeunt

Looking back at Act 4
Activities for groups or individuals

1 Dramatic range and scale

The three scenes of Act 4 contain great dramatic range:

- Ritual: the Witches around the cauldron
- Spectacle: the Apparitions and the show of eight kings
- Domestic family life: Lady Macduff and her son
- Horrific violation: the murders in Macduff's castle
- Deception and moral complexity: Malcolm's testing of Macduff
- Deep personal grief: Macduff hears of his family's slaughter.

a Try to reduce the dramatic range and scale of this act to a short text. As you do so, consider how each scene is juxtaposed to position the audience to understand the themes of the play.

b Write the script for a newsflash based on events in each scene. Try to limit your newsflash to 100 words.

c Create a haiku based on each scene. For example:

> Sheltered innocence,
> Object of ambitious greed:
> Gone, in one fell swoop.

2 A tempting letter from Macbeth

In Scene 3, Malcolm says that Macbeth has tried to lure him with offers of women, money and other incentives (lines 117–20). Write a letter from Macbeth, tempting Malcolm to return to Scotland.

3 'How many children had Lady Macbeth?'

'He has no children', cries Macduff in Scene 3 as he is advised to seek revenge on Macbeth. But in Act 1 Scene 7, Lady Macbeth says that she has suckled a child at her breast. The critic L. C. Knights wrote a famous essay titled 'How many children had Lady Macbeth?' His answer was that the question is unimportant, because *Macbeth* should be read as a dramatic poem rather than as a study of characters. Some productions of *Macbeth* have made 'children' a central concept. Does it matter, in the play, whether Lady Macbeth has children or not? How would you explain the significance of children, childlessness and violence against children as recurring ideas in this play?

4 Dramatic reading

a In groups, prepare a dramatic reading of an important passage relating to notions of kingship from Act 4 (at least ten lines). There are many ways in which each extract can be spoken and presented: consider tone, pauses, emphasis, speech, repetitions, movement, gesture and accompanying sound effects.

b List the various representations of kingship that are covered in this act. Include the positive and the negative and try to match each item with a relevant quotation.

5 Tableaux quotations

In groups, choose a key quotation from this act and present a physical representation of it for the rest of your class to guess the quotation. Give the class five clues as they try to guess your quotation.

6 Witchcraft and superstition

a In small groups, stage a mock trial of the Witches to determine the role they have played in Macbeth's destiny. Together, assemble a list of questions to ask them, then take turns to answer these questions in role as one of the Witches.

b Look at the photographs showing the Witches from different stage productions on the page opposite and at the end of Act 1. Write your opinions about the extent to which the Witches are to blame for what happens in the play. Include a description of how you would portray them on stage to convey your interpretation to the audience.

The Gentlewoman reports to the Doctor that she has seen Lady Macbeth sleepwalking. She refuses to tell what her mistress has said in her sleep. Lady Macbeth, asleep, enters with a candle.

1 The sleepwalking scene: act it out (in threes)

This is one of the most famous scenes in world drama.

a In groups of three, work out how you would stage it to maximum dramatic effect by preparing notes for the actors. Advise them on how they should speak and move, as well as what props you think they should use.

b Staying in your groups, experiment with ways of performing this scene, taking turns as Lady Macbeth. Remember to listen to the advice of the others in your group.

Write about it

What does Lady Macbeth write? (by yourself)

The Gentlewoman tells how she has seen Lady Macbeth carefully take paper, fold it, write on it, read it and seal it – all in her sleep. What do you think Lady Macbeth is writing? Is it a confession? A letter to Macbeth? A warning to Lady Macduff? Or something else? How honest might she be, bearing in mind that she is writing when she is unconscious? Write Lady Macbeth's letter, using modern English or imitating the prose used in this scene.

Themes

Obsessive Compulsive Disorder?

This scene is filled with unnatural and disturbed behaviour ('A great perturbation in nature'), so it is appropriate that Shakespeare wrote it in prose rather than verse. The language is uneven and lacking in the rich fluency of poetry. Lady Macbeth's obsessive washing of her hands, coupled with her sleepwalking, are telling signs of mental illness.

Find out some more about somnambulism and the illness known as Obsessive Compulsive Disorder (OCD). What causes these conditions? How might they be treated today? Report back to your class after you have learned more, focusing on the accuracy of Shakespeare's description.

DOCTOR OF PHYSIC doctor of medicine

WAITING-GENTLEWOMAN personal attendant

his majesty Macbeth

went into the field went to the battlefield

closet chest of valuables

seal to put a personal stamp in hot wax on a letter to ensure privacy and authenticity

effects appearances

watching waking

slumbery agitation sleepwalking

actual active

meet fitting

Neither to you … speech the Gentlewoman is unwilling to say what she has witnessed because she would be committing treason

taper candle

guise custom

close concealed

seem appear to be

set down write

Act 5 Scene 1
A room in Dunsinane Castle

Enter a DOCTOR OF PHYSIC, *and a* WAITING-GENTLEWOMAN

DOCTOR   I have two nights watched with you, but can perceive no truth in your report. When was it she last walked?

GENTLEWOMAN   Since his majesty went into the field, I have seen her rise from her bed, throw her night-gown upon her, unlock her closet, take forth paper, fold it, write upon't, read it, afterwards seal it, and again return to bed, yet all this while in a most fast sleep.

DOCTOR   A great perturbation in nature, to receive at once the benefit of sleep and do the effects of watching. In this slumbery agitation, besides her walking and other actual performances, what at any time have you heard her say?

GENTLEWOMAN   That, sir, which I will not report after her.

DOCTOR   You may to me, and 'tis most meet you should.

GENTLEWOMAN   Neither to you, nor anyone, having no witness to confirm my speech.

Enter LADY [MACBETH], *with a taper*

Lo you, here she comes. This is her very guise and, upon my life, fast asleep. Observe her, stand close.

DOCTOR   How came she by that light?

GENTLEWOMAN   Why, it stood by her. She has light by her continually, 'tis her command.

DOCTOR   You see her eyes are open.

GENTLEWOMAN   Ay, but their sense are shut.

DOCTOR   What is it she does now? Look how she rubs her hands.

GENTLEWOMAN   It is an accustomed action with her, to seem thus washing her hands; I have known her continue in this a quarter of an hour.

LADY MACBETH   Yet here's a spot.

DOCTOR   Hark, she speaks; I will set down what comes from her to satisfy my remembrance the more strongly.

5

10

15

20

25

Lady Macbeth, fast asleep, tries to wash imagined blood from her hands. Her fragmented language echoes her own and Macbeth's words about past murders: Duncan, Lady Macduff, Banquo.

Stagecraft

'will these hands ne'er be clean?'

Some modern productions (such as Polanski's movie) have highlighted the use of hands in *Macbeth* as a powerful motif that runs throughout the play. At times, the characters' hands seem almost removed from their bodies, acting separately to their wishes. Lighting can be employed very effectively to pick out actors' hands at key points in the play, as can film and projections.

How would you stage this scene so that the various actors' hands convey different emotions? Try storyboarding or filming to explore this aspect of the scene. Alternatively, create a tableau that emphasises the importance of hands.

1 Act out Lady Macbeth's dreams (in fives or sixes)

Lady Macbeth's sleepwalking language is dreamlike: short and disjointed recollections of Macbeth's deeds. There are twenty-six sentences in all. In groups, work on the script so that one of you speaks the lines and the other members of the group become other characters from the play. These might include King Duncan, Lady Macduff and her children, Banquo, the Witches, Malcolm, Donaldbain and Macbeth. As Lady Macbeth speaks, each character reacts using facial expressions, hand gestures and other forms of silent communication. Afterwards, talk together about the emotions you have explored as actors.

murky dark

Who knows … account Duncan's murder is not known because nobody can call the Macbeths to account

Thane of Fife Macduff

You mar … starting you spoil everything with your nervousness
Go to well, well (a remonstrance)

perfumes of Arabia spices

sorely charged heavily burdened

the dignity of the whole body the sake of life itself

practice professional ability, skill

on's on his

Directly immediately
Foul whisp'rings are abroad terrible rumours are circulating

divine priest

still always
mated confused

134

LADY MACBETH   Out, damned spot! Out, I say! One, two. Why 30
then 'tis time to do't. Hell is murky. Fie, my lord, fie, a soldier,
and afeard? What need we fear? Who knows it, when none can
call our power to account? Yet who would have thought the old
man to have had so much blood in him?

DOCTOR   Do you mark that? 35

LADY MACBETH   The Thane of Fife had a wife. Where is she
now? What, will these hands ne'er be clean? No more o'that,
my lord, no more o'that. You mar all with this starting.

DOCTOR   Go to, go to; you have known what you should not.

GENTLEWOMAN   She has spoke what she should not, I am sure of 40
that. Heaven knows what she has known.

LADY MACBETH   Here's the smell of the blood still; all the perfumes of Arabia will not sweeten this little hand. O, O, O.

DOCTOR   What a sigh is there! The heart is sorely charged.

GENTLEWOMAN   I would not have such a heart in my bosom for 45
the dignity of the whole body.

DOCTOR   Well, well, well –

GENTLEWOMAN   Pray God it be, sir.

DOCTOR   This disease is beyond my practice; yet I have known
those which have walked in their sleep who have died holily in 50
their beds.

LADY MACBETH   Wash your hands, put on your night-gown, look
not so pale. I tell you yet again, Banquo's buried; he cannot
come out on's grave.

DOCTOR   Even so? 55

LADY MACBETH   To bed, to bed; there's knocking at the gate.
Come, come, come, come, give me your hand; what's done
cannot be undone. To bed, to bed, to bed.   *Exit*

DOCTOR   Will she go now to bed?

GENTLEWOMAN   Directly. 60

DOCTOR   Foul whisp'rings are abroad; unnatural deeds
Do breed unnatural troubles; infected minds
To their deaf pillows will discharge their secrets.
More needs she the divine than the physician.
God, God forgive us all. Look after her; 65
Remove from her the means of all annoyance,
And still keep eyes upon her. So, good night,
My mind she has mated, and amazed my sight.
I think, but dare not speak.

GENTLEWOMAN   Good night, good doctor.

                                  Exeunt

Characters

'Those he commands, move only in command'
(by yourself, then whole class)

Macbeth's men are serving him not out of love and duty, but only because they have to. Many will desert him as the battle nears its end.

Imagine that you are one of Macbeth's soldiers. Write down three questions you would like to ask Macbeth as you consider your sense of duty to him as king. As a class, decide which question is the most important.

1 Hope! (in fours)

The four thanes are full of hope because of Macbeth's difficulties and the approach of Malcolm's army. They can see, not far ahead, freedom from tyranny. Speak lines 1–31 in two ways:

- Take parts as the four thanes and read through the scene.
- Do not take parts, but take turns to read up to a punctuation mark, then hand on. Speak in whispers, as conspirators.

Which reading most powerfully conveys a sense of mounting optimism?

Language in the play

Propaganda (in pairs)

The language Caithness and Angus use in lines 12–22 portrays Macbeth in a very negative way. Identify and write out three images from these lines that strongly capture their opinion of Macbeth. With a partner, talk about which image you think is the most powerful. Why did Shakespeare choose to describe Macbeth so negatively at this point in the play?

▶ Views of Macbeth: in pairs, one person reads the negative descriptions while the other mimes them.

Drum and colours drummer and flagbearer

Revenges ... man the cause that Malcolm and Macduff are fighting for is strong enough for a dying (or dead) man to rise up and join them

dear precious

bleeding running with blood

mortified dead

file list

unrough ... manhood unbearded young men, inexperienced in battle

buckle ... belt of rule keep his sick government in control by force

Now minutely ... faith-breach every minute there's a rebellion protesting against his treachery

When ... there Macbeth is at war with himself

med'cine ... weal Malcolm (the cure of the diseased kingdom)

purge cure by cleansing

Act 5 Scene 2
Scotland Open country

Drum and colours. Enter MENTEITH, CAITHNESS, ANGUS,
LENNOX, *Soldiers*

MENTEITH The English power is near, led on by Malcolm,
His uncle Siward, and the good Macduff.
Revenges burn in them, for their dear causes
Would to the bleeding and the grim alarm
Excite the mortified man.

ANGUS   Near Birnam Wood   5
Shall we well meet them; that way are they coming.

CAITHNESS Who knows if Donaldbain be with his brother?

LENNOX For certain, sir, he is not. I have a file
Of all the gentry; there is Siward's son
And many unrough youths that even now   10
Protest their first of manhood.

MENTEITH   What does the tyrant?

CAITHNESS Great Dunsinane he strongly fortifies.
Some say he's mad; others that lesser hate him
Do call it valiant fury, but for certain
He cannot buckle his distempered cause   15
Within the belt of rule.

ANGUS   Now does he feel
His secret murders sticking on his hands.
Now minutely revolts upbraid his faith-breach;
Those he commands, move only in command,
Nothing in love. Now does he feel his title   20
Hang loose about him, like a giant's robe
Upon a dwarfish thief.

MENTEITH   Who then shall blame
His pestered senses to recoil and start,
When all that is within him does condemn
Itself for being there?

CAITHNESS   Well, march we on   25
To give obedience where 'tis truly owed;
Meet we the med'cine of the sickly weal,
And with him pour we in our country's purge,
Each drop of us.

Macbeth, receiving news of desertions from his army, recalls the Apparitions' predictions. He rages at a soldier who tells of Malcolm's approach. He knows the coming battle will make or break him.

Stagecraft

The return of Macbeth (in threes)

This is our first sight of Macbeth since Act 4 Scene 1. In the previous scene, the thanes talk of how desperate he has become. In groups of three, plot Macbeth's rise and fall on a graph. When is he at his most successful and when is he at his lowest point? Share your work with the rest of the class. Do your graphs look similar to one another?

Characters

Macbeth's mood swings (in pairs)

Faced with bad news, Macbeth tries to cheer himself by recalling the words of the Apparitions ('Birnam Wood' and 'no man that's born of woman'). His mood was described in the previous scene as 'mad' or 'valiant fury', and his mood swings are evident in this scene.

a To help you understand Macbeth's varying moods, speak all he says in lines 1–61. Share his lines between you, speaking sentences alternately. Identify the points where Macbeth's mood and tone of voice change in the scene.

b Prepare notes for an actor playing Macbeth in this scene, advising him how he might speak.

1 'let them fly all' (in threes)

Macbeth hears of thanes who have deserted him to join the English forces, and he sees the fear in the face of the servant who brings him news of ten thousand English soldiers. It is clear that there are many who will not fight with Macbeth: they are either fighting against him or have fled in terror of the invading army.

Improvise Macbeth's servants discussing life at the castle. What have you witnessed since the king and queen were last seen in the play? What rumours have you heard about the English army?

---

dew the sovereign flower restore the rightful king

them the 'false thanes'

taint become infected, weaken

mortal consequences human destiny

epicures luxury-lovers

sway by rule, control

cream-faced pale

loon a villain or rogue

goose-look foolish appearance

over-red cover with red

lily-livered the liver was traditionally the organ of courage; here it is white and cowardly

linen white

counsellors advisers

whey-face milky, pale with fear

Seyton possibly pronounced as 'Satan' and therefore a reference to demonic power

push attack

cheer … disseat me comfort me or dethrone me

LENNOX
Or so much as it needs
To dew the sovereign flower and drown the weeds.   30
Make we our march towards Birnam.

Exeunt, marching

Act 5 Scene 3
Dunsinane Castle

Enter MACBETH, DOCTOR, *and Attendants*

MACBETH
Bring me no more reports, let them fly all;
Till Birnam Wood remove to Dunsinane,
I cannot taint with fear. What's the boy Malcolm?
Was he not born of woman? The spirits that know
All mortal consequences have pronounced me thus: 5
'Fear not, Macbeth, no man that's born of woman
Shall e'er have power upon thee.' Then fly false thanes
And mingle with the English epicures;
The mind I sway by and the heart I bear
Shall never sag with doubt nor shake with fear.   10

Enter SERVANT

The devil damn thee black, thou cream-faced loon.
Where got'st thou that goose-look?

SERVANT
There is ten thousand –

MACBETH
Geese, villain?

SERVANT
Soldiers, sir.

MACBETH
Go prick thy face and over-red thy fear,
Thou lily-livered boy. What soldiers, patch?   15
Death of thy soul, those linen cheeks of thine
Are counsellors to fear. What soldiers, whey-face?

SERVANT
The English force, so please you.

MACBETH
Take thy face hence!

[Exit Servant]

Seyton! – I am sick at heart,
When I behold – Seyton, I say! – this push   20
Will cheer me ever or disseat me now.

Macbeth reflects on a bleak future. He determines to fight to the death, and orders rumour-mongers to be killed. When the Doctor tells him he cannot cure mental disorders, Macbeth dismisses medicine.

Characters

Not 'honour' but 'mouth-honour' (in pairs)

Macbeth wearily broods on the unhappy future that awaits him. In line 25 he lists four things that old people hope for, and in lines 27–8 two things he is likely to receive. Actors try to speak such 'lists' using a different tone of voice for each 'item'.

In pairs, explore Macbeth's innermost thoughts. One person speaks the lines and the other improvises deeper reflections that are unspoken in the play. Take it in turns to do this and then compare your approaches.

1 'a mind diseased'

The language Macbeth uses in lines 41–6 is rich in metaphor and is both lyrical and tender. Try to sketch out the metaphors in these lines, visualising the rich imagery. Discuss your work with the rest of the class, explaining what you hoped to capture in your sketches. You could add your work to the wall displays you are developing on *Macbeth*.

Write about it

Lady Macbeth: her psychoanalyst's report

Three hundred years before Sigmund Freud, Shakespeare seems to have invented psychoanalysis. Macbeth's description of 'a mind diseased' (line 41) exactly captures the anxiety, depression and sorrow that Freud sought to cure by psychoanalysis. Freud's method (sometimes known as 'the talking cure') resembles what the Doctor says in line 46–7: 'Therein the patient / Must minister to himself.' This expresses the heart of psychoanalytic practice: the patient, by talking through his or her problem with an analyst, effectively finds his or her own cure.

Imagine that you are Lady Macbeth's analyst writing a final report of all the meetings you have had with her. What questions have you asked and what answers were you given? What do you think is the cause of her illness and how might it be cured? Include a transcript from some of your meetings with her, your own analysis of her illness, and your suggested ways of treating it in your final report.

---

way course

sere dry and withered

yellow leaf autumn (metaphorically the period just before death)

troops flocks, crowds

stead place

mouth-honour, breath lip service, flattery

fain gladly

horses warriors mounted on horseback

skirr scour

sick physically sick (as distinct from psychologically ill)

thick-coming fancies frequent nightmares

minister to cure

Raze out the written troubles erase the deep anxieties

physic medicine

dispatch hurry up

cast / The water analyse the urine

pristine fresh, original

I have lived long enough. My way of life
Is fall'n into the sere, the yellow leaf,
And that which should accompany old age,
As honour, love, obedience, troops of friends,   25
I must not look to have; but in their stead,
Curses, not loud but deep, mouth-honour, breath
Which the poor heart would fain deny, and dare not.
Seyton!

Enter SEYTON

SEYTON   What's your gracious pleasure?

MACBETH   What news more?   30

SEYTON   All is confirmed, my lord, which was reported.

MACBETH   I'll fight till from my bones my flesh be hacked.
Give me my armour.

SEYTON   'Tis not needed yet.

MACBETH   I'll put it on;   35
Send out more horses; skirr the country round.
Hang those that talk of fear. Give me mine armour.
How does your patient, doctor?

DOCTOR   Not so sick, my lord,
As she is troubled with thick-coming fancies
That keep her from her rest.

MACBETH   Cure her of that.   40
Canst thou not minister to a mind diseased,
Pluck from the memory a rooted sorrow,
Raze out the written troubles of the brain,
And with some sweet oblivious antidote
Cleanse the stuffed bosom of that perilous stuff   45
Which weighs upon the heart?

DOCTOR   Therein the patient
Must minister to himself.

MACBETH   Throw physic to the dogs, I'll none of it.
Come, put mine armour on; give me my staff. –
Seyton, send out. – Doctor, the thanes fly from me. –   50
[*To Attendant*] Come sir, dispatch. – If thou couldst, doctor, cast
The water of my land, find her disease,
And purge it to a sound and pristine health,
I would applaud thee to the very echo

Macbeth leaves, calling for his armour. The Doctor determines to desert. Malcolm orders the army to use branches to camouflage their approach to Dunsinane. He reports many desertions from Macbeth's army.

Stagecraft

The coming of Birnam Wood (by yourself)

The approaching forces decide to camouflage themselves by using branches cut from Birnam Wood. How would you stage something this big in a theatre? Write notes to the cast of the play, advising them how this might be done successfully. Suggest the props they should use, as well as sound effects and lighting.

▼ This is how a 2011 production showed Malcolm's army advancing, holding branches from Birnam Wood. Work out how, in your own production, you could stage the approach of the camouflaged army.

cynne senna, a plant to purge (cleanse) the body

bane ruin

Profit money (doctors were thought of as greedy in Shakespeare's time)

chambers bedrooms (Duncan was murdered in his bedroom)

shadow conceal

discovery / Err in report of us military reconnaissance reports are wrong about our numbers

setting down before't lay siege to

advantage to be given opportunities to escape

more and less ... revolt nobles and ordinary soldiers have deserted Macbeth

constrainèd things unwilling conscript soldiers

That should applaud again. – Pull't off, I say! –   55
What rhubarb, cynne, or what purgative drug
Would scour these English hence? Hear'st thou of them?

DOCTOR   Ay, my good lord; your royal preparation
Makes us hear something.

MACBETH   Bring it after me. –
I will not be afraid of death and bane,   60
Till Birnam Forest come to Dunsinane.

                          [*Exeunt all but Doctor*]

DOCTOR   Were I from Dunsinane away and clear,
Profit again should hardly draw me here.   *Exit*

Act 5 Scene 4
Near Birnam Wood

Drum and colours. Enter MALCOLM, SIWARD, MACDUFF,
Siward's son, MENTEITH, CAITHNESS, ANGUS, *and* SOLDIERS,
marching

MALCOLM   Cousins, I hope the days are near at hand
That chambers will be safe.

MENTEITH   We doubt it nothing.

SIWARD   What wood is this before us?

MENTEITH   The Wood of Birnam.

MALCOLM   Let every soldier hew him down a bough,
And bear't before him; thereby shall we shadow   5
The numbers of our host and make discovery
Err in report of us.

A SOLDIER   It shall be done.

SIWARD   We learn no other, but the confident tyrant
Keeps still in Dunsinane and will endure
Our setting down before't.

MALCOLM   'Tis his main hope,   10
For where there is advantage to be given,
Both more and less have given him the revolt,
And none serve with him but constrainèd things
Whose hearts are absent too.

Siward advises against over-optimism. Macbeth defies the siege. Only desertions stop him openly facing Malcolm's army. He has almost lost any sense of fear. Seyton brings news of Lady Macbeth's death.

Stagecraft

Scene contrast, speech contrast

Scene 4 dramatically contrasts with Scene 3. Macbeth's reliance on the Apparition's forecast that he would not be defeated until Birnam Wood came to Dunsinane is followed by Malcolm's order to his soldiers to cut branches from Birnam Wood as camouflage. Now Shakespeare ends Scene 4 with Macduff's calm call for 'Industrious soldiership', then provides an immediate contrast by opening Scene 5 with Macbeth's defiant bravado.

As you read on, make a note of other contrasts that increase the dramatic tension, such as scene length and atmosphere.

1 'I have supped full with horrors' (in pairs)

The sound of women mourning prompts Macbeth to reflect that he has lost almost all sense of fear. Once, an owl's shriek or a horror story would make his blood run cold and his hair stand on end.

a What has caused Macbeth to change? Discuss this in pairs and consider if you think it makes him more or less vulnerable.

b Take turns to speak lines 9–15 in such a way that brings out the differences in tone from Macbeth's first speech in this scene.

Characters

'The queen, my lord, is dead' (in pairs)

How did Lady Macbeth die? At the end of the play, Malcolm reports that she committed suicide, but that may not be true (because history is written by the victors). Talk together about how you think she might have met her death, then *either* write her farewell letter *or* write an obituary for a newspaper in which you give an account of her life and her death.

just censures … event rightful claims decide the result

owe own, have won

Thoughts … arbitrate thinking won't determine the matter, but battle will

ague fever

forced reinforced

dareful defiant

beard to beard face to face, hand-to-hand combat

my fell of hair every hair on my body

treatise story

supped full with horrors metaphorically: filled up with horrors; literally: have eaten with Banquo's ghost

Direness horror

slaughterous murderous

start frighten

MACDUFF   Let our just censures
           Attend the true event and put we on   15
           Industrious soldiership.
SIWARD   The time approaches
           That will with due decision make us know
           What we shall say we have and what we owe;
           Thoughts speculative their unsure hopes relate,
           But certain issue strokes must arbitrate.   20
           Towards which, advance the war.

Exeunt, marching

Act 5 Scene 5
Dunsinane Castle

Enter MACBETH, SEYTON, *and Soldiers, with drum and colours*

MACBETH   Hang out our banners on the outward walls;
           The cry is still, 'They come.' Our castle's strength
           Will laugh a siege to scorn; here let them lie
           Till famine and the ague eat them up.
           Were they not forced with those that should be ours,   5
           We might have met them dareful, beard to beard,
           And beat them backward home.
                      A cry within of women
                                    What is that noise?
SEYTON   It is the cry of women, my good lord.
MACBETH   I have almost forgot the taste of fears;
           The time has been, my senses would have cooled   10
           To hear a night-shriek and my fell of hair
           Would at a dismal treatise rouse and stir
           As life were in't. I have supped full with horrors;
           Direness familiar to my slaughterous thoughts
           Cannot once start me. Wherefore was that cry?   15
SEYTON   The queen, my lord, is dead.

His wife's death sets Macbeth brooding on life's futility. A messenger tells that Birnam Wood is moving towards Dunsinane. Macbeth doubts the Apparition's ambiguous words. He determines to die fighting.

Characters

'Tomorrow, and tomorrow, and tomorrow' (in pairs)

In lines 18–27, Macbeth wearily speaks of time past, present and future, and of how fragile and empty he finds life. Ultimately, he says, it means 'nothing'. This is a profound contemplation about life, and it is worth studying it in depth. Work on one or more of the following:

- Speak the lines in different ways (perhaps sadly or wonderingly).
- Whisper the lines to each other, as though telling a secret.
- Emphasise the bleak fatalism of the words.
- Decide who Macbeth is speaking to (Himself? Seyton? The audience? Or someone else?)
- Devise actions and expressions for each section.
- Talk together about the imagery Macbeth uses. What makes it so powerful?

Themes

Fate and free will (in pairs)

The Messenger's announcement that he has seen Birnam Wood raises issues relating to the theme of fate and free will. To what extent do you think Macbeth has control of his fate? Can he alter how he might die and who might kill him?

Script an imaginary dialogue between two students of your own age discussing these issues, with one student arguing that Macbeth is in control and the other arguing that he is not. Remember to use specific examples from the play's events and characters.

1 What does it mean to be brave? (by yourself)

Macbeth is a play preoccupied with what it means to be brave, and each of the main characters has the opportunity to prove their courage in many different ways (even the Messenger, a minor character, has to be brave to tell Macbeth the news about Birnam Wood).

Write two or three paragraphs arguing for the character you think is the bravest of all, using specific references from the play to support your argument.

She … word there are two possible meanings for this line: if Lady Macbeth had died later there would have been time to mourn her, or Lady Macbeth would have inevitably died later

petty small, insignificant

syllable the smallest part

recorded written down

Out, out perhaps a reference to Lady Macbeth's taper (candle) in Act 5 Scene 1

poor player bad actor

frets worries

report relate

watch period of guard duty

cling wither

sooth true

I pull in resolution I lose my firmness of purpose

equivocation lies, double-talk

the fiend the Third Apparition

avouches says is true

tarrying waiting

'gin begin

th'estate o'th'world the universe, the ordered world

wrack destruction

harness armour

MACBETH   She should have died hereafter;
                    There would have been a time for such a word.
                    Tomorrow, and tomorrow, and tomorrow
                    Creeps in this petty pace from day to day
                    To the last syllable of recorded time;   20
                    And all our yesterdays have lighted fools
                    The way to dusty death. Out, out, brief candle,
                    Life's but a walking shadow, a poor player
                    That struts and frets his hour upon the stage
                    And then is heard no more. It is a tale   25
                    Told by an idiot, full of sound and fury
                    Signifying nothing.

                              Enter a MESSENGER

                    Thou com'st to use thy tongue: thy story quickly.
MESSENGER   Gracious my lord,
                    I should report that which I say I saw,   30
                    But know not how to do't.
MACBETH   Well, say, sir.
MESSENGER   As I did stand my watch upon the hill
                    I looked toward Birnam and anon methought
                    The wood began to move.
MACBETH   Liar and slave!
MESSENGER   Let me endure your wrath if't be not so;   35
                    Within this three mile may you see it coming.
                    I say, a moving grove.
MACBETH   If thou speak'st false,
                    Upon the next tree shall thou hang alive
                    Till famine cling thee; if thy speech be sooth,
                    I care not if thou dost for me as much.   40
                    I pull in resolution and begin
                    To doubt th'equivocation of the fiend
                    That lies like truth. 'Fear not, till Birnam Wood
                    Do come to Dunsinane', and now a wood
                    Comes toward Dunsinane. Arm, arm, and out!   45
                    If this which he avouches does appear,
                    There is nor flying hence nor tarrying here.
                    I 'gin to be aweary of the sun
                    And wish th'estate o'th'world were now undone.
                    Ring the alarum bell! Blow wind, come wrack;   50
                    At least we'll die with harness on our back.

                                                            Exeunt

Malcolm instructs his troops to throw aside their camouflage of branches. He issues orders for battle. Macbeth compares himself to a baited bear. He is challenged by Young Siward.

Stagecraft

'harbingers of blood and death' (in threes)

Act 5 Scene 6 is a short, transitional scene of only ten lines. Some filmmakers have used these battle scenes to show the vast scale of the conflict. Theatre directors have to operate with more limitations, including the fact that the actors should be camouflaged with branches. Discuss how you would stage this scene:

- in your school hall or theatre
- in an open-air theatre
- in a big-budget movie.

Now collate your ideas and choose the best (and most workable) of them to write up as advice to a director, outlining how this scene could be staged effectively.

Themes

Appearance and reality (in pairs)

In Act 4 Scene 3, Malcolm appears to Macduff to be something he is not; here, he asks his soldiers to discard their branches and 'show like those you are'. The difference between appearance and reality is important in *Macbeth*.

Discuss the key episodes in the play that illustrate the difference between appearance and reality. Talk about why you think Shakespeare and his audience were so fascinated by the interplay between the two. Extend this discussion by talking with other pairs about whether modern society is equally preoccupied with such issues.

1 Shakespearean sports

Macbeth's reference to being trapped like a baited bear would have created a very powerful image for Shakespeare's audiences. Sports such as bear-baiting and cock-fighting were popular in the area where the Globe was situated. Find out about the sports and other amusements that the audience might have walked past on their way to the theatre. What do these sports tell us about the society of the time, and to what extent have things changed since then? Present your research to others in the class orally, or in the form of posters. These could be displayed to build up a picture of Elizabethan and Jacobean life.

leafy screens branches

clamorous harbingers noisy forerunners (trumpet blasts)

Alarums continued by keeping the sounds of the battle continuous, the audience knows that it is moving to another part of the battlefield, not moving to a different time

Near the castle gate the scene takes place either just outside or inside Dunsinane Castle

tied chained
stake post
course battle, period of trial

Act 5 Scene 6
Outside Dunsinane Castle

Drum and colours. Enter MALCOLM, SIWARD, MACDUFF, *and
their army, with boughs*

MALCOLM   Now near enough; your leafy screens throw down
      And show like those you are. You, worthy uncle,
      Shall with my cousin your right noble son
      Lead our first battle. Worthy Macduff and we
      Shall take upon's what else remains to do,   5
      According to our order.

SIWARD   Fare you well.
      Do we but find the tyrant's power tonight,
      Let us be beaten if we cannot fight.

MACDUFF   Make all our trumpets speak; give them all breath,
      Those clamorous harbingers of blood and death.   10

Exeunt

Alarums continued

Act 5 Scene 7
Near the castle gate

Enter MACBETH

MACBETH   They have tied me to a stake; I cannot fly,
      But bear-like I must fight the course. What's he
      That was not born of woman? Such a one
      Am I to fear, or none.

Enter YOUNG SIWARD

YOUNG SIWARD   What is thy name?   5

MACBETH   Thou'lt be afraid to hear it.

YOUNG SIWARD   No, though thou call'st thyself a hotter name
      Than any is in hell.

Macbeth kills Young Siward and boasts that no man born of woman can kill him. Macduff refuses to fight with mercenaries and seeks only Macbeth. Siward invites Malcolm to enter Macbeth's surrendered castle.

Stagecraft

'My name's Macbeth' (in pairs)

This is a very dramatic moment in the scene: Macbeth is clearly aware that his name will strike terror into the hearts of many. Some directors use this as an opportunity to show just how invulnerable Macbeth is to all those soldiers 'born of woman', leading up to the killing of Young Siward. How do you think Macbeth should appear at this point in the play? Does he feel untouchable, or is he deranged and increasingly desperate? Discuss the different ways this might be staged.

1 'Let me find him, Fortune' (in threes)

On the battlefield, Macduff eagerly searches for Macbeth. Explore Macduff's motives for seeking out the king and discuss how he should act. One person plays 'Revenge', arguing that Macduff should be merciless; another plays 'Forgiveness', arguing that Macbeth should be treated leniently. The third person is Macduff himself, listening to these arguments. How does he respond in each case? Swap roles to bring out different perspectives.

2 'The tyrant's people on both sides do fight' (in pairs, then by yourself)

Some of Macbeth's soldiers have deserted and now fight for Malcolm (line 26). In pairs, write some notes for and against defecting from Macbeth's forces. Using these notes, step into role as a soldier and write a private letter to a close friend, explaining why you have chosen to either defect or fight. What are your views of Macbeth? Of Scotland? Of your future happiness and ambition? (Try to refer to the conversation between Malcolm, Macduff and Ross in Act 4 Scene 3, lines 140–79 to develop the personal reasons for your actions.)

abhorrèd detested

whose arms ... staves mercenaries (who fight only for money)

staves wooden weapons

unbattered undamaged

undeeded unused (having performed no deeds)

There where there is most noise

one of greatest note Macbeth

bruited shouted about

gently rendered surrendered with little fighting

strike beside us deliberately miss us or fight beside us

MACBETH   My name's Macbeth.

YOUNG SIWARD   The devil himself could not pronounce a title
                More hateful to mine ear.

MACBETH   No, nor more fearful.   10

YOUNG SIWARD   Thou liest, abhorrèd tyrant; with my sword
                I'll prove the lie thou speak'st.

Fight, and young Siward slain

MACBETH   Thou wast born of woman.
                But swords I smile at, weapons laugh to scorn,
                Brandished by man that's of a woman born.

Exit [with young Siward's body]

Alarums. Enter MACDUFF

MACDUFF   That way the noise is. Tyrant, show thy face!   15
                If thou be'st slain, and with no stroke of mine,
                My wife and children's ghosts will haunt me still.
                I cannot strike at wretched kerns whose arms
                Are hired to bear their staves; either thou, Macbeth,
                Or else my sword with an unbattered edge   20
                I sheath again undeeded. There thou shouldst be;
                By this great clatter, one of greatest note
                Seems bruited. Let me find him, Fortune,
                And more I beg not.   *Exit*

Alarums. Enter MALCOLM *and* SIWARD

SIWARD   This way, my lord; the castle's gently rendered. 25
                The tyrant's people on both sides do fight;
                The noble thanes do bravely in the war.
                The day almost itself professes yours,
                And little is to do.

MALCOLM   We have met with foes
                That strike beside us.

SIWARD   Enter, sir, the castle.   30

Exeunt

Alarum

Facing Macduff, Macbeth boasts that no naturally born man can kill him, but Macduff reveals his own Caesarean birth. Dismayed, Macbeth refuses to fight. Macduff threatens he will be exhibited in captivity.

Characters

'play the Roman fool' (in pairs)

With his men deserting him and his castle taken, Macbeth must realise that he has lost the battle. But he rejects the idea of committing suicide ('play the Roman fool') and is determined to fight on, reminding us of the Captain's speech in Act 1 Scene 2, in which he depicts Macbeth as a warrior at heart. Debate which position is the more persuasive: one person argues that Macbeth is foolish, the other that he is admirable. Refer closely to Macbeth's words.

1 Who is the most guilty? (in small groups)

In the previous scene, Macduff admits that he feels guilty for the death of his wife and children (Act 5 Scene 7, line 17). Here, Macbeth admits that he feels guilty for the death of Macduff's family ('my soul is too much charged / With blood of thine already'). But how different are their crimes? In groups, put each character on trial, with a prosecution, defence and judge. You may wish to consider:

• how their crimes are morally different
• why Shakespeare allows us to see this side of their characters
• how our view of both characters changes with these admissions.

2 'Despair thy charm'

Macbeth has been relying on the prophecy that he cannot be killed by 'one of woman born'. Macduff's revelation that he was not born naturally, but by Caesarean section, shatters Macbeth. He realises he has been duped by the Witches and their equivocations. Suggest how Macbeth physically reacts to Macduff's revelation and how he delivers lines 17–22.

Themes

Macbeth's guilt (whole class)

The threat of being displayed in a cage in a circus is a humiliation that Macbeth cannot bear to contemplate. What ten crimes of Macbeth's would you write beneath Macduff's proposed sign? As a class, decide on everything he is guilty of, then sequence his crimes in order of importance, with the most serious at number one.

---

play the Roman fool commit suicide (defeated Roman generals fell on their swords)

lives living beings

charged weighted

terms words

Thou losest labour you waste effort

intrenchant uncuttable

keen sharp

impress mark

crests helmets, heads

angel devil, Satan

Untimely ripped prematurely delivered (by Caesarean section)

cowed intimidated

my better part of man most of my courage

juggling cheating

palter us in a double sense equivocate with double meanings

keep ... hope there is a difference between prophesying kingship and fulfilling it, and I now see this

yield thee coward admit that you are a coward

Act 5 Scene 8
Outside Dunsinane Castle

Enter MACBETH

MACBETH   Why should I play the Roman fool and die
On mine own sword? Whiles I see lives, the gashes
Do better upon them.

Enter MACDUFF

MACDUFF   Turn, hell-hound, turn.

MACBETH   Of all men else I have avoided thee,
But get thee back, my soul is too much charged   5
With blood of thine already.

MACDUFF   I have no words;
My voice is in my sword, thou bloodier villain
Than terms can give thee out.

Fight. Alarum

MACBETH   Thou losest labour.
As easy mayst thou the intrenchant air
With thy keen sword impress as make me bleed.   10
Let fall thy blade on vulnerable crests;
I bear a charmèd life which must not yield
To one of woman born.

MACDUFF   Despair thy charm,
And let the angel whom thou still hast served
Tell thee, Macduff was from his mother's womb   15
Untimely ripped.

MACBETH   Accursèd be that tongue that tells me so,
For it hath cowed my better part of man;
And be these juggling fiends no more believed
That palter with us in a double sense,   20
That keep the word of promise to our ear
And break it to our hope. I'll not fight with thee.

MACDUFF   Then yield thee coward,
And live to be the show and gaze o'th'time.
We'll have thee, as our rarer monsters are,   25
Painted upon a pole and underwrit,
'Here may you see the tyrant.'

Macbeth determines to go down fighting, and is killed. Siward reports light casualties. On being told that his son is dead, Siward's concern is to know if Young Siward died bravely.

Characters

'I will not yield' (in pairs)

Lines 27–34 are Macbeth's last lines in the play, and here he chooses life over death. With a partner, discuss how he would give this speech then act out different ways of delivering the lines. Think about the last impression of Macbeth you want to leave with the audience: is his death brave and dignified, or cowardly and abject?

1 The death of a dictator

The death of a dictator is always a public (and political) act. Find out how ancient tyrants met their deaths: King Ahab and Queen Jezebel (pictured below), Andronicus I, or, from the modern era, look at how the Romanian dictator Nicolae Ceauşescu died, or King Faisal II of Iraq, or the Italian leader Benito Mussolini, as well as more contemporary examples. Do their deaths have any similarities with Macbeth's? Share your thoughts with the rest of the class.

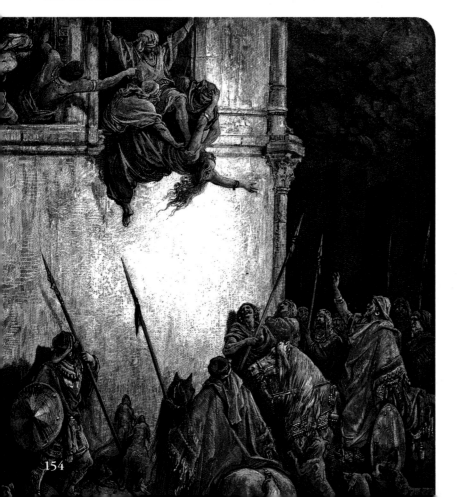

To kiss the ground to surrender
baited mocked, tormented like a chained bear
rabble crowd, the general public
try the last go on to the end

Hold, enough! stop, surrender

Retreat, and flourish. trumpet call at the end of battle, fanfare

go off die

soldier's debt death

prowess bravery

brought off the field taken from the battlefield for burial

Had he his hurts before? were his wounds on the front of the body? (Was he facing the enemy not running away?)

MACBETH   I will not yield
To kiss the ground before young Malcolm's feet
And to be baited with the rabble's curse.
Though Birnam Wood be come to Dunsinane   30
And thou opposed being of no woman born,
Yet I will try the last. Before my body,
I throw my warlike shield. Lay on, Macduff,
And damned be him that first cries, 'Hold, enough!'
                                        Exeunt[,] fighting. Alarums

Enter [Macbeth and Macduff,] fighting[,] and Macbeth slain

[Exit Macduff, with Macbeth's body]

Act 5 Scene 9
Dunsinane Castle

Retreat, and flourish. Enter with drum and colours, MALCOLM,
SIWARD, ROSS, *Thanes, and Soldiers*

MALCOLM   I would the friends we miss were safe arrived.
SIWARD   Some must go off. And yet by these I see,
          So great a day as this is cheaply bought.
MALCOLM   Macduff is missing and your noble son.
ROSS   Your son, my lord, has paid a soldier's debt;   5
          He only lived but till he was a man,
          The which no sooner had his prowess confirmed
          In the unshrinking station where he fought,
          But like a man he died.
SIWARD   Then he is dead?
ROSS   Ay, and brought off the field. Your cause of sorrow   10
          Must not be measured by his worth, for then
          It hath no end.
SIWARD   Had he his hurts before?
ROSS   Ay, on the front.

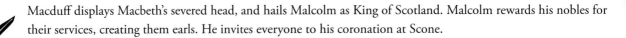

Macduff displays Macbeth's severed head, and hails Malcolm as King of Scotland. Malcolm rewards his nobles for their services, creating them earls. He invites everyone to his coronation at Scone.

Themes

'I would not wish them to a fairer death' (whole class)

Siward shows such a lack of feeling for his dead son that even Malcolm seems surprised and promises to mourn him as well ('He's worth more sorrow, / And that I'll spend for him'). Do you think Siward is being brave here, or uncaring? As a class, talk about the different representations of bravery in *Macbeth*. Who shows true courage and when, and who is cowardly? The discussion would benefit from forward planning and research: think about the issues involved, and the possible arguments that might be made by other members of the class.

1 The restoration of peace? (in pairs)

In most of his tragedies, Shakespeare aims to restore a sense of peace and natural order to society by the end of the play. Here, Malcolm seems to emphasise such restoration by rewarding his allies and asking for the exiled to return. Do you think Malcolm deserves to be king? Knowing what you know about him, and Scotland at the time, do you think he will be a good king? Discuss this in pairs and then take forward your ideas to the next activity.

2 The final curtain (in large groups)

Create a tableau that captures the new hierarchy in Scotland. Where would you place Malcolm, Ross and Macduff (and where would Macbeth's head be placed)? You might want to bring back key players in the future of Scotland, such as Donaldbain and Fleance. If there is more than one group in your class, compare your tableaux and question each group on why it chose its arrangement.

3 Bring on the Witches (in small groups)

Some productions of the play have the Witches present at these final moments of the play. In one, they attended on Malcolm, marking him out as a future victim. In another, they hovered over the dead body of Macbeth – the victim they had enticed to disaster. Work out your own presentation of lines 21–42, and include the Witches to make some comment about Macbeth or the future of Scotland.

knell is knolled death bell is rung

paid his score settled his account (died bravely)

Hail a word of praise, but one used by the Witches to greet Macbeth, and by Macbeth in his soliloquy in Act 3 Scene 1, line 61; thus Malcolm is linked with Macbeth

compassed ... kingdom's pearl surrounded by the nobility of Scotland

reckon with your several loves calculate what I owe each of you

make us even settle our accounts

earls a new title in Scotland, and perhaps a reference to King James, who did the same when he became King of England and Ireland

be planted newly ... time begin the new era

exiled friends friends who fled abroad

watchful tyranny Macbeth's totalitarian regime

ministers supporters

by self ... life took her own life

grace of Grace grace of God

measure the right amount

SIWARD   Why then, God's soldier be he;
Had I as many sons as I have hairs,   15
I would not wish them to a fairer death.
And so his knell is knolled.

MALCOLM   He's worth more sorrow,
And that I'll spend for him.

SIWARD   He's worth no more;
They say he parted well and paid his score,
And so God be with him. Here comes newer comfort.   20

Enter MACDUFF, *with Macbeth's head*

MACDUFF   Hail, king, for so thou art. Behold where stands
Th'usurper's cursèd head. The time is free.
I see thee compassed with thy kingdom's pearl,
That speak my salutation in their minds;
Whose voices I desire aloud with mine.   25
Hail, King of Scotland.

ALL   Hail, King of Scotland.

Flourish

MALCOLM   We shall not spend a large expense of time
Before we reckon with your several loves
And make us even with you. My thanes and kinsmen,
Henceforth be earls, the first that ever Scotland   30
In such an honour named. What's more to do
Which would be planted newly with the time, –
As calling home our exiled friends abroad
That fled the snares of watchful tyranny,
Producing forth the cruel ministers   35
Of this dead butcher and his fiend-like queen,
Who, as 'tis thought, by self and violent hands
Took off her life, – this and what needful else
That calls upon us, by the grace of Grace
We will perform in measure, time, and place.   40
So, thanks to all at once and to each one,
Whom we invite to see us crowned at Scone.

Flourish

                     Exeunt

FINIS

Looking back at the play
Activities for groups or individuals

1 The big moments

What are the key scenes in *Macbeth*? In large groups, pick out the pivotal moments in the play by choosing what you think are the most important lines. Try to condense each act to between twenty and thirty lines; remember, you can cut out lines but you must not alter Shakespeare's language. Now assign parts to each member of the group and think about how you might stage these condensed acts. Ideally, your group will be divided into five smaller groups and each should work on one act. Afterwards, bring them together for a short, focused, blast of *Macbeth* as a whole.

2 Arranging a press conference

Arrange a table with Malcolm, Macduff, Ross, and Siward facing the media after the final battle has taken place. Each member of the 'press pack' should think of questions to ask about what has just happened; questions should be directed at the group and at specific individuals. Write down the answers and then, in groups, put the stories together: choose the medium you want to use to report on this conference (newspaper, radio, television, website blog or something else). You may want to take an editorial line in advance (pro-Malcolm or pro-Macbeth). Now discuss the answers as a class and explore why the various reports were similar and different.

3 Mini-*Macbeth*

Write a summary of *Macbeth* in exactly one hundred words. Then cut that down to exactly seventy-five words (try to stick to complete sentences); then cut that down to exactly fifty words. Continue to do this until you get it down to ten words. Now share these words with the class: you can post these on a designated pinboard, or use sticky notes, or put them on a class website. Discuss the choices made. Select one word that you think captures the most important element in the play.

4 Preparing for your production

How would you move *Macbeth* from being a 'flat text' to a successful performance? Over the course of studying the play, you have come up with many ideas. Now try to bring these together into one consolidated resource for a group of actors who are about to start rehearsing for a production. In addition to your notes to actors and directors, add other essential documents: a letter to potential financial sponsors (why should they invest in it?); posters; advertisements for print and web-based media; a strategy paper for promoting the production via social media; illustrations for the set design, props and costumes.

5 Debate: is Macbeth a tragic hero or, as Malcolm says, 'a butcher'?

In his final speech, Malcolm refers to Macbeth as a 'butcher'. But is he? Copy and complete a table similar to the one below, which outlines the qualities that a tragic hero has, and those that are more closely associated with a butcher.

Butcher	Tragic hero
Ruthless	Having a weakness
Unsympathetic	Sympathetic (feels guilt, shows emotions)

Organise a whole-class debate on this question. Think about the quotations you wish to use to support your points. Make sure you choose a chairperson who will bring in as many different views as possible.

Perspectives and themes

What is the play about?

Imagine that you can travel back in time to around 1606. You meet William Shakespeare a few minutes after he has finished writing *Macbeth*. You ask him 'What is the play about?' But, like all great artists, Shakespeare doesn't seem interested in explaining his work. He leaves that up to others. He seems to say: 'Here it is. Read it, perform it, make of it what you will.'

There has been no shortage of responses to that invitation! *Macbeth* has been hugely popular ever since it was first performed. The thousands of productions and millions of words written about it show that there is no single 'right way' of thinking about or performing the play. You will probably have noticed this as you looked at the photographs of different productions in this book.

The play is like a kaleidoscope. Every time it is performed it reveals different shapes, patterns, meanings, interpretations. For example, you could think about *Macbeth* as:

• a play of political and social realism, which shows how an oppressive hierarchical society produces corrupt individuals

• a tragedy in which a great man falls because of a fatal flaw in his character (Macbeth's ambition causes his death)

• a historical thriller with many elements of a fast-moving, action-packed murder story

• a moral tale advising against regicide (the murder of a king); remember, this would have pleased James I

• a psychological study of a murderer's mind, in which Macbeth constantly reveals his troubled innermost thoughts.

There are also various interpretive standpoints that allow different 'readings' of the play. People have interpreted *Macbeth* according to a number of perspectives. These include:

Feminist perspectives – looking at the way women are represented

Cultural materialist perspectives – looking at the way politics, wealth and power strongly influence every human relationship

New historicist perspectives – focusing on the repressive conditions of Shakespeare's own time

Psychoanalytical perspectives – looking at the unconscious and the irrational, as well as the impact of repressed sexuality and desire

Liberal humanist perspectives – freedom and human progress are the goals of life, and final reconciliation and harmony are possible

◆ In pairs, talk about which of the perspectives described above would be most helpful in exploring *Macbeth* further. Then, either individually or together, write the script for a dialogue between two people with different perspectives on the play. Try to show how their conversation develops, and encourage them to agree or disagree with each other about the meaning of *Macbeth*.

Themes

Another way of answering the question 'What is *Macbeth* about?' is to identify the themes of the play. Themes are ideas or concepts of fundamental importance that recur throughout the play, linking together plot, characters and language. Themes echo, reinforce and comment upon each other – and the whole play – in interesting ways. For example, it is hard to write about appearance and reality in the play without referring to the manifestation of evil or the hidden dangers beneath a pleasing exterior. It is equally difficult to write about kingship and masculinity without talking about the themes of loyalty and ambition.

As you can see, themes are not individual categories but a 'tangle' of ideas and concerns that are interrelated in complex ways. In your writing you should aim to explore the way these themes cross over and illuminate each other, rather than simply listing each of the themes.

You might also like to think about the way the themes work at different levels: the individual level (psychological or personal); the social level (linked to society and nation); and the natural level (the natural or supernatural world). For example, in *Macbeth* you can clearly see how the theme of appearance and reality works across all three of these levels.

The themes of *Macbeth* include the following:

Ambition – the ruthless seeking of power by Macbeth, urged on by his equally ambitious wife. It can be thought of as the tragic flaw that causes his downfall ('I have no spur / To prick the sides of my intent, but only / Vaulting ambition').

Evil – the brooding presence of murderous intention, destroying whatever is good. Macbeth's conscience troubles him, but he commits evil, and finds others to carry out his malign orders (the murders of Duncan, Banquo, Lady Macduff).

Order and disorder – the struggle to maintain or destroy social and natural bonds; the destruction of morality and mutual trust ('Uproar the universal peace, confound / All unity on earth').

Appearance and reality – evil lurks behind fair looks. Deceit and hypocrisy mean that appearances cannot be trusted. The theme occurs throughout. It is introduced in the first scene as the Witches chant 'Fair is foul, and foul is fair'. Later, in Act 1 Scene 5, Lady Macbeth urges Macbeth to 'look like th'innocent flower, / But be the serpent under't'.

Equivocation – telling half-truths with the intention to mislead ('th'equivocation of the fiend / That lies like truth').

Violence and tyranny – warfare, destruction and oppression recur throughout the play. In the first scene, the Witches speak of 'the battle', and in the second, the wounded Captain reports Macbeth's victory in a bloody war.

Tempted by the prospect of becoming king, Macbeth embarks on a violent journey that makes him Scotland's tyrant. Malcolm expresses the theme with the words: 'Pour the sweet milk of concord into hell.'

Guilt and conscience – Macbeth knows what he does is wrong, but he does it nonetheless and suffers agonies of conscience as a result ('O, full of scorpions is my mind').

Masculinity – the violent feudal society of hierarchical male power breeds bloody stereotypes of what it is to be a man. 'I dare do all that may become a man', says Macbeth, contemplating murder. But the play offers other visions of manhood: 'But I must also feel it as a man', cries Macduff, weeping at news of his family's murder.

◆ Working in small groups, devise a tableau that shows one of the themes of the play. Present your tableau, frozen for one minute, for other groups to guess which theme is being portrayed.

◆ Imagine you are asked to explain what *Macbeth* is about by an eight-year-old child, and also by your teacher/lecturer. Write a reply to each of them, using these two pages to help you.

161

The contexts of *Macbeth*

One way of thinking about *Macbeth* is to set it in the context of its time: the world that Shakespeare knew. His dramatic imagination was influenced by many features of that world. Layers of dramatic possibilities within the script are built on past performances (such as miracle and morality plays), other literary texts (such as Holinshed's *Chronicles*) and contemporary events or topical concerns (such as the accession of James to the throne and the general interest in witchcraft at the time). This layering gives Shakespeare's plays great depth without limiting them to any single or specific social, religious or political meaning.

Writing for a king

In 1603, James, King of Scotland and a member of the Stuart dynasty, succeeded Queen Elizabeth I on the English and Irish thrones. Some critics argue that Shakespeare wrote *Macbeth* partly to flatter the new king (who probably saw a performance in 1606), and that he deliberately included many references to events and issues that would have interested James.

The play has a large focus on kingship, ideas of succession and the health of the nation. *Macbeth* explores the qualities of a good king and the horrors of living in a country ruled by a tyrant. Issues of power and politics are raised through the play's exploration of the sacred power and divine right of kings, the nature of lawful succession, the relationship between England and Scotland, and the dangers of treason and sedition.

Macbeth refers to the hanging of traitors and to the Gunpowder Plot of 5 November 1605. The king's escape from being blown up was commemorated by a medal showing a snake concealed by flowers. The Plot may be referred to in Act 2 Scene 3, line 50 ('dire combustion'). Sir Everard Digby, one of the conspirators, was a favourite of James (and possibly mirrored by the treacherous Thane of Cawdor). The play's concern with equivocation may also refer to Henry Garnet, who was accused of treason for involvement in the Gunpowder Plot. He was found to have committed perjury (lying on oath), but in self-defence claimed to have the right to equivocate.

Equivocation is the use of deliberately misleading half-truths; it was seen as a diabolical use of language that distorted the truth and damned men's souls to hell. Equivocation is a major theme of the play and Macbeth is frequently troubled by it, fearing that the Witches may have lied to him.

▼ **The execution of Henry Garnet.**

The theme of kingship and ideas of what makes a good king run through the play. In the activities throughout this book, you have had opportunity to consider Macbeth as a political leader. At times it is also possible to compare him to a warrior like Braveheart, especially in Act 1 Scene 2. Further comparisons can be made between Macbeth and historical tyrants, such as Joseph Stalin and Idi Amin.

◆ Draw a table with two columns. In the first column, list all the qualities of a tyrant. In the second column, list Macbeth's qualities. To what extent does he fit the criteria of a bloody tyrant?

Witches and witchcraft

Throughout Shakespeare's life, during the reigns of Elizabeth I and James I, many people suspected of being witches were cruelly persecuted, and those who were convicted faced the prospect of being burned to death. Hundreds of pamphlets describing the lurid details of many witchcraft trials were printed. They enjoyed enormous sales: the equivalent of today's popular newspapers, or movies and books about the supernatural.

Witches were credited with diabolical powers. For example, they could predict the future, fly, sail in sieves, bring on night in daytime, cause fogs and tempests, and kill animals. In Act 1, the First Witch describes how she created a storm to destroy the captain of the *Tiger*. The *Tiger* was a real ship that set sail from England in 1604 and undertook a disastrous voyage on its way to Japan. After suffering storms and navigational errors, it finally returned to England around the time Shakespeare was writing this play. Although the voyage of the *Tiger* was a real event, Shakespeare was more interested in the dramatic and imaginative possibilities of attributing this disaster to witchcraft and spells.

It was also thought that witches cursed their enemies with fatal wasting diseases, induced nightmares and sterility, and could take demonic possession of others. People believed that witches allowed the Devil to suck their blood in exchange for a 'familiar': a bird, reptile or beast as an evil servant. Accused witches were examined for the 'Devil's mark': a red mark on the body from which Satan had sucked blood (some of Shakespeare's audience might have interpreted Lady Macbeth's 'damned spot' as evidence of the Devil's mark). Many of those watching *Macbeth* saw in the play the signs of a man and woman seized by demonic possession: disturbed behaviour, lack of fear and indifference to life. Both Macbeth and Lady Macbeth fall into trances, have strange visions and invite evil spirits to possess their bodies.

King James was as fascinated by witchcraft as any of his subjects. In 1590, a group of witches tried to kill him by raising a storm to sink his ship. Their plot was discovered and they were brought to trial at North Berwick. James personally interrogated Dr Fian, a key witness during the trials. The poor doctor was horribly tortured:

> *His nails upon all his fingers were riven and pulled off … his legs were crushed and beaten together as small as might be, and the bones and flesh so bruised that the blood and marrow spouted forth in great abundance.*

Fired by his experience of the trial, King James personally investigated other witchcraft cases and, in 1597, published *Demonologie*, a book on witchcraft. In 1604, an Act of Parliament decreed that anyone found guilty of witchcraft should be executed.

◆ The paragraphs above describe how people in Shakespeare's day understood witchcraft and witches. They also describe how Shakespeare alluded to many of the ideas about evil, the demonic and kingship that preoccupied James I. Re-read this information, then write an opinion article for a local newspaper giving a different perspective on witchcraft and witches. Try to explain why Shakespeare might have included witches in his play about a tyrant-king who murders his way to the throne. Do you think he was influenced by contemporary hysteria about the diabolical powers of witches when he was writing *Macbeth*?

Shakespeare's reading

As he wrote *Macbeth*, Shakespeare had at his side a book published in 1587: *Chronicles of England, Scotland and Ireland* by Raphael Holinshed. Shakespeare had earlier used Holinshed's *Chronicles* extensively as the source for his English History plays. Now, he found in it the Scottish stories that his imagination would turn into the drama of *Macbeth*. But Shakespeare never slavishly followed any source. Holinshed provided details of events, power politics, characters and motivations. Shakespeare selected, altered and added to them to achieve maximum dramatic effect. Here is an extract from Holinshed's *Chronicles*:

> *It fortuned as Macbeth and Banquo journied towards Forres, where the King then lay, they went sporting by the way together without other company save only themselves, passing through the woods and fields, when suddenly in the midst of a land, there met them three*

women in strange and wild apparel, resembling creatures of elder world, whom when they attentively beheld, wondering much at the sight, the first of them spake and said: All hail Macbeth, thane of Glamis (for he had lately entered into that dignity and office by the death of his father Sinel). The second of them said: Hail Macbeth, thane of Cawdor. But the third said: All hail Macbeth that hereafter shall be King of Scotland.

As well as writing in dramatic form, Shakespeare invented Lady Macbeth's sleepwalking and death, the banquet scene and Banquo's Ghost, and most of the cauldron scene. He also vividly portrayed the changing relationship between Macbeth and Lady Macbeth. He made Lady Macbeth a key character in his story, whereas Holinshed only made a brief comment about her as 'very ambitious, burning in unquenchable desire to bear the name of queen'. Unlike Holinshed, Shakespeare did not make Banquo an accomplice to Duncan's murder. Instead, he made the Macbeths solely responsible. This alteration presumably pleased King James because he hated regicides (king-killers) and because he believed he was a descendant of the historical Banquo. See the table below for a summary of the way Shakespeare changed Holinshed's account of *Macbeth*.

Holinshed	Shakespeare
Duncan is an ineffectual king	Duncan is a respected and revered ruler
Macbeth reigns for ten years as a good ruler	Macbeth is a tyrant immediately after he becomes king
Lady Macbeth is described in passing	Lady Macbeth has great prominence in the play
Banquo is an accomplice to Duncan's murder	Banquo is an innocent victim murdered by Macbeth

◆ Step into role as William Shakespeare. Write out what went through your mind as you rewrote Holinshed. Remember, as a playwright you are always asking yourself: 'How can I put this on stage to greatest dramatic effect?'

Mystery plays and morality plays

Shakespeare doesn't limit *Macbeth* to the themes or characteristics of medieval plays, but he does remind his audience of these earlier dramatic traditions. He invites them to make connections and activates their experiences of past traditions to bring greater depth to their understanding of *Macbeth*.

Some critics claim that *Macbeth* shows Shakespeare's recollection of mystery plays, which were dramatised Bible stories immensely popular as entertainment and instruction in the Middle Ages. The mystery play *The Harrowing of Hell* is thought to be the inspiration for the Porter scene in *Macbeth*. In it, Hell is a castle whose gate is guarded by a Porter named Rybald ('ribald' means coarse and vulgar). Christ descends to Hell and hammers on the gate, demanding that Satan release the good souls imprisoned there. In this interpretation of the play, Macduff is the Christ-like figure who knocks at Macbeth's castle door. In Act 5, he enters the castle, kills the devil-tyrant, redeems Scotland and leads its people from darkness into light. Macbeth is singled out as the man who turns his castle and the whole of Scotland into

▼ The Day of Judgement, from the Guild Chapel in Stratford-upon-Avon. As a schoolboy, Shakespeare must have seen this painting often.

a type of hell, and Macduff is identified as Scotland's avenger and rescuer, through this reference to *The Harrowing of Hell*.

Medieval morality plays portrayed the human struggle to choose between vice and virtue. They personified a range of Vices (including the seven deadly sins) and Virtues in stories of temptation and conflict between good and evil. The hero, often given a generic name like Everyman or Mankind, must choose between them. Although the Everyman figure is led astray by the Vice figure, and wallows in sinfulness, he repents and is saved at the end of the play. The point of the plays is that although the hero succumbs to sin, God's mercy is always available to one who repents. In this way, the morality plays made the basic elements of Christianity accessible to those who were unable to read the Latin Bible for themselves. They taught people to watch out for the common vices that might tempt them and to have faith in the mercy of God.

◆ Use the information above to give a context-based alternative interpretation of *Macbeth*. Consider how Shakespeare might have been influenced by medieval religious drama. You might like to reflect on how Macbeth could be seen as an Everyman figure, tempted to evil by different Vices and heading towards either heaven or hell in the course of the play. Also consider whether the link between Macduff and Christ or Macbeth and the devil-tyrant intensifies the conflict between them.

◆ Write a short letter to a younger student telling them about an alternative interpretation of *Macbeth* based on this information. You might like to do more research as you write this letter.

Tragedy

Tragedies were popular in Shakespeare's England. They dramatised the fall from power of kings, princes and military leaders and the way this affected the fortunes of states and nations. Tragedies contained assassination, bloodshed and revenge, and were written to instruct as well as to entertain. Shakespeare was influenced by the Roman playwright Seneca (4 BC–AD 65), whose tragedies included soliloquies, ghosts, witches, magic, violent events, wrongs avenged and moral statements.

Shakespeare was also influenced by the development of tragedy as a dramatic form in England. The most significant aspect of this development was the focus on the protagonist, who was responsible for his own downfall and often displayed a fatal flaw or essential trait that contributed to his death. Elizabethan and Jacobean tragedy contained sub-plots, spectacle and onstage violence. They also depicted a movement towards isolation and social breakdown – an inevitable sequence of events that led ultimately to the death of the protagonist (and many of the other characters).

◆ Find out more about Elizabethan tragedies and the trajectory of the protagonist towards isolation, chaos and death. How would you plot Macbeth's trajectory? Create a diagram or a graph that charts this trajectory. Beneath it write a description of the characteristics that might contribute to the fatal flaw or essential trait that propels Macbeth towards his downfall. How does this add to your understanding of the play?

Characters

How are characters created?

The process of creating and developing characters is called 'characterisation'. In *Macbeth*, Shakespeare does this in three major ways:

By their actions – Macbeth murders Duncan; then he has Banquo and Lady Macduff and her family murdered.

By what is said about them – amongst other things, Lady Macbeth is called 'fiend-like'; Macbeth is called 'brave' several times, as well as a 'butcher'.

Through their own language – how they speak with each other and, through **soliloquy**, what they say to themselves when alone.

Each of these is equally important. Soliloquies allow us to gain a deep insight into the innermost thoughts of the speaker, but other characters provide us with different views, and their actions are these words made real. Every character has a distinctive voice, and part of Shakespeare's genius is to explore each aspect while allowing that voice to both change (as events affect the character's mind) and remain unique and recognisable.

The Lady Macbeth we see in Act 5 Scene 1, although recognisably the same character from Act 1 Scene 5, has changed profoundly, and we learn this from her words ('Here's the smell of the blood still; all the perfumes of Arabia will not sweeten this little hand. O, O, O'), her actions (the sleepwalking, the obsessive hand-washing) and what is said about her by the Gentlewoman and the Doctor ('I would not have such a heart in my bosom for the dignity of the whole body').

◆ Which speeches by both characters offer the greatest insight into them? Collect key quotations about these characters and the way they change in the course of the play. Display your choice of quotations on a large piece of paper, with images that symbolise these significant moments.

◆ In small groups, discuss how Macbeth and Lady Macbeth change over the course of the play. Which of their actions most influence how you view them? What comments made by other characters about Macbeth and Lady Macbeth tell us most about them?

Macbeth

Although there are exciting moments in the play, much of the drama takes place in Macbeth's mind. He struggles with good and evil, and believes that his fate is decided by the Witches and other sinister forces. When trying to understand Macbeth, it helps to think about how a performer might approach playing the role: what might the actor feel are the motives that drive Macbeth to act in the way he does?

Below are some views of Macbeth by actors who have played the part and by a director. Read through them, then talk with a partner about which you think is the most striking view.

It was Macbeth as a poet, as the creator of a new vision, rather than as a soldier or a king, that I found most intriguing and mysterious. Charting the progress of a man who redefines himself as he analyses his experience became, for me, the single most important and interesting challenge.

Simon Russell Beale

In the last Act he [Macbeth] does, in my view, reach nobility, clarity and strength, a sense of the reality of the consequences of actions.

Sir Peter Hall

[He is] a killing machine with an elegant turn of phrase.

Jonathan Pryce

I went through the play marking the times he speaks of fear, particularly in relation to himself. He does so in every scene: it is paramount for him; the man is constantly fearful … The moment before he does the murder he is afraid – the dagger speech is a fearful speech, the utterance of a terrified man. He does the murder for her, and it destroys them both.

Derek Jacobi

I see Macbeth as ambitious but capable of darkness. The witches saw something in him, they picked the right person. Witches plus Macbeth equals evil. Was evil there before though, I'm not sure you can say. Is anyone evil without input from others?

Liam Brennan

◆ **Rank these quotations in order, with the one that most closely matches your understanding of Macbeth at the top.**

◆ **In small groups, and then with the rest of your class, discuss which of these comments gives you the greatest insight into the character of Macbeth.**

Macbeth appears first in the play as a military hero. King Duncan calls him 'valiant cousin, worthy gentleman', 'noble Macbeth', 'worthiest cousin'. He ends the play as a cruel tyrant, deserted by his soldiers and allies, and finally slain by Macduff. The new king, Malcolm, viewing Macbeth's severed head, dismisses him as 'this dead butcher'.

It is easy to characterise Macbeth as a common murderer, but he is more complex than this – and he changes radically throughout the play. Paradoxically, perhaps, the more he kills, the more aware he becomes of the futility of his actions and even of life itself. Macbeth is revealed as a deeply sensitive man, tortured by his imagination and his conscience. His wife believes him to be a good, and even gentle, man ('too full o'th'milk of human kindness') and he knows that it is wrong to kill Duncan. He struggles to overcome his evil thoughts, but is tempted to criminality by the Witches, by his wife's pressure, and by his own ambition. He murders his way to the throne of Scotland, and then arranges the killing of anyone he suspects to be his enemy.

Conflicting thoughts of good and evil constantly torment Macbeth ('O, full of scorpions is my mind, dear wife!'). But as he is drawn ever deeper into cruel and brutal actions, he strives to harden his responses and to lose 'the taste of fears'. Learning of his wife's death, he reflects despairingly on the emptiness of life, saying that it is 'a tale / Told by an idiot, full of sound and fury / Signifying nothing'.

He finally becomes aware that the Witches have misled him ('be these juggling fiends no more believed'). Even in his despair and weariness he determines to die bravely ('Blow wind, come wrack; / At least we'll die with harness on our back'). He slays Young Siward and, coming face to face with Macduff, still fights defiantly to the end although he realises he has met his nemesis ('Lay on, Macduff, / And damned be him that first cries, "Hold, enough!"'). Whether Macbeth's final words and actions represent heroic endurance or the snarling of a trapped animal is open for each reader or new performance to decide.

Lady Macbeth

For many actors and directors, Lady Macbeth is as difficult to define as her husband: she undergoes profound changes over the course of the play, and can be seen as a fiend or a supportive, ambitious wife.

◆ Just as you did with Macbeth, read the comments below and rank them in order, with the one you feel is closest to the truth as number one. After you have done this, discuss them in groups and then with the rest of your class.

She had no illusions about the evil she was embracing, but the thrill of it drew her back.

Judi Dench

And then she sees the blood ... something happens to her gut. For her, the sight is horrible. It shocks her, the reality of it ... After that we began talking different languages. We who had needed to touch each other all the time grew distant. When he had killed, neither of us wanted to touch each other.

Sinead Cusack

I think first and foremost she's a wife, she's a homemaker, she's a very, very intelligent woman. I think that the audience have to have an affection for this woman to be able to see how far she and her husband fall. I think she's a very strong woman who's the backbone, the crutch of Macbeth. In their marriage she's been the backbone of him.

Allison McKenzie

Lady Macbeth appears first as a supremely confident, dominant figure. She revels in the prospect of Macbeth becoming king, and calls on evil spirits to help her persuade him to kill Duncan. She urges him to use deception to cloak murderous intentions ('look like th'innocent flower, / But be the serpent under't').

When Macbeth's resolve to carry out the murder weakens, she ridicules his masculinity, convincing him to do the deed. She becomes his active accomplice, even returning the bloody daggers to Duncan's bedroom. It is the murder of Duncan that brings the Macbeths most closely together; however, this is also the moment that they begin to move irrevocably apart.

From this point, Lady Macbeth's decline seems inevitable. In Act 3, she begins to feel the emptiness of their achievement, seeing only 'doubtful joy'. She appears increasingly isolated and drained of energy as Macbeth moves away from her into his own troubled thoughts. She becomes more of an audience to Macbeth's words, rather than his partner. Although she rallies at the disastrous banquet, she ends that scene displaying none of her earlier dominance over her husband. Shakespeare does not show Lady Macbeth's decline into nervous breakdown and death, giving only one glimpse of that horrifying process: the torment she experiences in her sleepwalking. She dies off stage, an anti-climax of an event that seems to mark out her decline even more sharply.

◆ Study the pictures of Macbeth and Lady Macbeth in this section. Discuss in groups what each of these pictures conveys about the characters. In the same groups, choose one of the following activities:

a *Hot-seating* One person steps into role of Macbeth. Group members ask him questions about why he did what he did. You can do the same with another person taking the role of Lady Macbeth.

b *A modern duologue* In pairs, write a duologue between Macbeth and Lady Macbeth reflecting on their actions and trying to explain their behaviour; or if you prefer, improvise this instead of writing a script. Other members of your group watch and give feedback, commenting on how true to the spirit of both characters the interpretations are.

c *Essay planning* Every member of the group writes one essay question each on:

- Macbeth
- Lady Macbeth
- their relationship.

The group chooses the strongest question and plans an answer collectively. Deliver your essay plans as a presentation to the rest of the class. Keep the presentation succinct, using between six and eight slides (each slide representing a different part of the essay). Each slide should contain only key words: it's up to the group to talk the class through the answer in more detail.

The language of *Macbeth*

Imagery

Imagery is the use of emotionally charged words and phrases that conjure up vivid mental pictures. These words, phrases and images are a kind of verbal painting that stirs the imagination, deepens dramatic impact and gives insight into character.

Macbeth is full of striking visual images. After the disastrous appearance of Banquo's Ghost at the banquet, and knowing that Macduff has turned against him, Macbeth resolves to commit yet more murders: 'I am in blood / Stepped in so far that should I wade no more, / Returning were as tedious as go o'er' (Act 3 Scene 4, lines 136–8). He sees himself wading through a river of blood and is so far in that it does not matter whether he goes on or turns back.

Sometimes an image extends over several lines. For example, in Act 1 Scene 7, lines 25–8, Macbeth soliloquises about whether or not to kill King Duncan, and concludes with an image from horse-riding:

> I have no spur
> To prick the sides of my intent, but only
> Vaulting ambition which o'erleaps itself
> And falls on th'other –

In this image of rider and horse, Macbeth sees himself like a horseman who urges on his mount by digging his spurs into the horse's sides. But he has no such motivation ('spur') to kill Duncan other than 'Vaulting ambition': like a rider vaulting on to his horse, but misjudging his leap and collapsing in failure on the other side.

Examples of how the imagery of the speeches and soliloquies can be illustrated with appropriate pictures can be seen in movies. In Polanski's film of *Macbeth*, for example, a bear-baiting post is used at several points in the play to emphasise the bear-baiting image.

◆ In role as a film director, write out your ideas for how the imagery in certain passages might be visualised in a film production. Prepare a screenplay or script to illustrate your ideas.

Recurring imagery

Macbeth is rich in imagery and certain images recur through the play, contributing to its distinctive atmosphere.

Blood

Images of blood carry great emotional force in *Macbeth*. The play begins and ends with bloody battles, and much blood is shed throughout, from that of 'blood-boltered Banquo' to Lady Macduff and her children. Macbeth is obsessed with blood and imagines himself wading through a river of blood, while Lady Macbeth, sleepwalking, smells blood and tries to rub away the spot of blood on her hands.

Darkness

Much of the action takes place at night, and the frequent images of darkness create a pervasive sense of evil. The Witches' presence and their spells and incantations heighten this, as does Lady Macbeth's invocation of evil spirits and darkness in Act 1.

Theatre

Shakespeare's fascination with his own profession provided him with a recurring theme: the world as a stage. On this stage, humans make brief, insignificant appearances to play their parts. Macbeth uses imagery relating to acting and theatre when he hears of the death of his wife in Act 5 Scene 5:

> Life's but a walking shadow, a poor player
> That struts and frets his hour upon the stage
> And then is heard no more.

Falconry and bear-baiting

Falconry (the art of training and hunting with a falcon) was also used as a key image by Shakespeare. Macbeth calls on 'seeling night' to come and 'Scarf up the tender eye of pitiful day', referring to the practice of sewing up hawks' eyes during the training process. Macduff describes the death of his wife and children in 'one fell swoop', referring to the way a falcon descends on its prey.

The bear-baiting that Shakespeare saw near the Globe Theatre also inspired an image for Macbeth as he is surrounded by his enemies and facing death at the end of the play:

> They have tied me to a stake; I cannot fly,
> But bear-like I must fight the course.

Disease

The Witches' 'fog and filthy air' in the first scene begins the imagery of sickness. This continues in references to the poison that goes in their cauldron and the 'infected' air they ride on. Disease and sickness affects both Scotland, 'the sickly weal', and the Macbeths – Lady Macbeth has a 'mind diseased' and Macbeth describes his mind as 'full of scorpions'.

Nature

Frequent images of animals, birds and insects are often ominous, and there are recurring images of ferocious creatures. Shakespeare shows how evil overruns Scotland by using images of nature disturbed.

◆ Choose one example of recurring imagery in the play and collect as many pictures from magazines or the Internet as you can that represent this. Find quotations from the play that link to the images you have chosen, then think of an appropriate way to display them, such as in a collage.

Metaphor, simile and personification

Shakespeare's imagery uses metaphor, simile and personification. All are comparisons.

A **simile** compares one thing to another using 'like' or 'as'. Macbeth challenges Banquo's Ghost to approach 'like the rugged Russian bear'; the First Witch threatens the sailor she will 'drain him dry as hay'.

A **metaphor** is also a comparison, suggesting that two dissimilar things are actually the same. Donaldbain says 'There's daggers in men's smiles'.

Personification is a special kind of imagery that turns all kinds of things into persons, giving them human feelings or attributes. The bleeding Captain speaks of Macbeth as 'Valour's minion' (bravery's favourite) and of 'Fortune' smiling on the rebel Macdonald. In Act 4, Scotland is described as weeping, diseased and suffering under the evil rule of Macbeth.

▼ Imagery of blood recurs throughout the play. After murdering Duncan, Macbeth wonders 'Will all great Neptune's ocean wash this blood / Clean from my hand?'. Later, Lady Macbeth asks 'will these hands ne'er be clean?'

Verse and prose

Shakespeare's audiences expected tragedies to be written in verse, because verse was thought to be appropriate to great men, affairs of state, and moments of emotional or dramatic intensity.

Macbeth is written mainly in **blank verse**, which is unrhymed lines that have carefully placed stressed and unstressed syllables. Each line has five feet (groups of syllables) called iambs, each of which has an unstressed (×) and stressed (/) syllable that sounds like a heartbeat (da DUM, da DUM, da DUM, da DUM, da DUM):

```
×    /   ×    /   ×   /  ×    /  ×   /
So foul and fair  a day I  have not seen.
```

The Witches almost always speak in four-beat rhythm (tetrameter), a style appropriate to spells, incantations and the supernatural. The rhythm is the opposite of the heartbeat rhythm described above (DUM-da, DUM-da, DUM-da, DUM-da):

```
  /      /        /     /
Fair is foul, and foul is fair
```

Shakespeare uses a varied rhythmic pattern throughout the play. He sometimes wrote lines of more or fewer than ten syllables, sometimes changed the pattern of stresses in a line, and sometimes used rhyming couplets for effect. He ensured that the rhythm of the verse was appropriate to the meaning and mood of the speech: reflective, fearful, apprehensive, anguished or confused.

These rhythmic patterns are what distinguish verse from prose, not whether they rhyme. Prose is different from blank verse: it is everyday language with no specific rhythm, metric scheme or rhyme. Shakespeare uses prose to break up the verse in his plays, to signify characters' madness or low status, or to draw attention to changes in plot or character. It is easy to tell the difference: verse passages begin with a capital letter and the lines do not reach the other side of the page, whereas prose passages have lines that reach both sides of the pages and only use capital letters at the beginning of sentences.

Shakespeare also used **caesura** and **enjambement** to add to the rhythm of his blank verse. A caesura is where the phrasing of the line is broken to create a pause or a break in the dialogue or action. With enjambement, the end of one sentence carries over into the next line of poetry, giving the impression that the phrases are spilling over and building up from one line to the next.

◆ **The human heartbeat is the rhythm of iambic pentameter. Put your hand on your heart to hear the basic rhythm of weak and strong stresses.**

◆ **Choose a verse speech. Explore ways of speaking it to emphasise the metre (four or five beats). For example, you could clap hands, tap the desk or walk five paces to accompany each line. Then write eight or more lines of your own in the same style.**

Antithesis and repetition

Antithesis is the opposition of ideas, words or phrases against each other. It expresses the conflict that is at the heart of the play. In 'When the battle's lost, and won' and 'Fair is foul, and foul is fair' the conflict is shown in 'lost' against 'won', 'fair' against 'foul'. Antithesis is especially powerful in *Macbeth*, where good is set against evil and where deception and false appearances are major themes.

Shakespeare used **repetition** to give his language great dramatic force. Repeated words, phrases, rhythms and sounds add to the emotional intensity of a scene. This repetition can occur on many levels:

Repetition of words Sometimes the same word is repeated in a short space of time in order to increase pace and tension. The following exchange between the Witches illustrates this:

Show!
Show!
Show!
Show his eyes and grieve his heart

At other times a word is repeated throughout a passage so that the idea can be developed or extended:

Still it cried, 'Sleep no more' to all the house;
'Glamis hath murdered sleep', and therefore Cawdor
Shall sleep no more: Macbeth shall sleep no more.

Repetition of sounds Alliteration is the repetition of consonants (at the beginning of words): 'Fair is foul, and foul is fair' and 'Double, double toil and trouble'. **Assonance** is the repetition of vowel sounds (in the middle of words):

Thrice to thine, and thrice to mine,
And thrice again, to make up nine.

These repetitions are opportunities for actors to intensify emotional impact. Rhyming couplets, which often end long speeches in blank verse or signal the end of a scene, also show this repetition of sound:

*Hear it not Duncan, for it is a **knell**,*
*That summons thee to heaven or to **hell**.*

Repetition of patterns Anaphora is the repetition of the same word at the beginning of successive sentences:

***Though** bladed corn be lodged and trees blown down,*
***Though** castles topple on their warders' heads,*

Epistrophe is the repetition of a word or phrase at the end of a series of sentences or clauses:

*When you durst do it, then **you were a man**.*
*And to be more than what **you were**, you would*
*Be so much more the **man**.*

Polyptoton is repetition of words derived from the same root word, but with different endings or forms:

*But yet I'll make **assurance** double **sure***
And take a bond of fate

◆ Turn randomly to any two or three pages of *Macbeth* and identify all the ways in which Shakespeare uses repetition on those pages. Try out different ways of speaking the lines to discover how emphasising or playing down the repetition can contribute to dramatic effect.

Soliloquies and asides

A **soliloquy** is a monologue, a kind of internal debate spoken by a character who is alone (or assumes they are alone) on stage. It gives the audience direct access to the character's mind, revealing their inner thoughts and motives. Macbeth often 'thinks aloud', expressing doubt,

fear, guilt and confusion. His soliloquy in Act 5 Scene 5 conveys his overwhelming despair, and in Act 1 Scene 5, Lady Macbeth's soliloquy is an impassioned appeal for demonic spirits to possess her.

An **aside** is a brief comment or address to the audience that shows the character's unspoken thoughts, unheard by other characters on stage. The audience is taken into this character's confidence or can see deeper into their motivations and experiences. Asides can also be used for characters to comment on the action as it unfolds.

◆ Identify some of the play's soliloquies and asides. Choose one and write notes on how you would speak it on stage to maximise dramatic effect.

◆ Copy and complete the table below as a summary of the information in this section.

Quotation	Language use	Its effect and meaning
'Fair is foul, and foul is fair'	Antithesis	The tension and confusion in this antithesis adds to the evil atmosphere and the sense of foreboding in the whole scene.

Macbeth in performance

Performance on Shakespeare's stage

Many people believe that because of the references to the Gunpowder Plot of 1605, *Macbeth* was first written and performed in 1606 as a tribute to King James I (who was also King James VI of Scotland). The first record of a production was written by Simon Forman, who described a performance he saw at the Globe Theatre on Bankside in 1611. Many of Shakespeare's plays were performed at the Globe, one of the many specially designed outdoor playhouses built at the end of the sixteenth century. They were modelled on the public amphitheatres like the bear-baiting rings that existed in the seedier locations outside the city walls (and the city's jurisdiction).

During Shakespeare's lifetime, plays in outdoor amphitheatres like the Globe were performed in broad daylight during the summer months. So, at 2.00 p.m. people would assemble with food and drink to watch a play with no lighting and no rule of silence for the audience. There were high levels of background noise and interaction during performances, and audience members were free to walk in and out of the theatre.

In the Globe, the audience was positioned on three sides of the stage: the 'groundlings' stood in the pit around the stage, while those who paid more were seated in three levels around the pit. Actors would see around three thousand faces staring up or down at them. The positioning of the audience made it difficult for everyone to hear all that was going on. Inevitably the actors would have their backs to sections of the audience at times. The best place for an actor to stand, especially for a soliloquy or an aside, was at the front of the stage, so that he could directly address almost all of the audience. However, it would be tedious if all the action occurred there!

Shakespeare's use of repetition helped to overcome this problem. Sometimes the same idea is stated or developed in three ways, to allow an actor to address each section of the audience. These repetitions were never simply word-for-word, but were used to create rhythm, accumulate details and build on an idea through different metaphors and imagery. If you spot significant repetition, it may be a clue that Shakespeare intended the character to move around the stage to engage the audience.

▼ This map from 1647 shows the Globe Theatre (the circular building, centre left), built for the second time in 1614 after the first one burnt down. It was mistaken by the artist Wenceslaus Hollar for a bear-baiting pit that was nearby.

◆ Look at some of Macbeth's and Lady Macbeth's soliloquies and identify where repetition might allow an actor to use the stage space in different ways. Imagine you are on the Globe stage and read out the lines while addressing different parts of your (imaginary) audience. Experiment with other ways of enacting repetition of words or ideas in the soliloquy for dramatic effect.

Shakespeare included many other clues for his actors in his play scripts. These clues are known as 'embedded stage directions' because of the coded instructions they gave to the actors about who to talk to, when to move or gesture and when to exit. Clues about setting, weather, clothing, other characters' appearances and onstage action were also placed in the scripts. In Act 4, when Macbeth sees the Apparitions, eight kings and the Ghost of Banquo, his dramatic exclamations can also be seen as embedded stage directions so that the actor knows how to respond: 'A fourth? Start, eyes!' His words a few lines later could also prompt the actor playing Banquo's Ghost (or prompt the imagination of the audience if no Ghost is present): 'the blood-boltered Banquo smiles upon me, / And points at them for his.'

Embedded stage directions were invaluable for early modern actors, who had little time to rehearse and not much opportunity to study the whole play before a performance. When a play was written, a scribe would make a copy. This was then cut up and each actor was given a scroll with his speeches stitched together along with basic cues and stage directions. The actors would memorise their lines, taking particular care that they knew their cues so they would understand when to enter and speak. A summary of the play, known as a 'backstage plot', was hung up backstage, so actors would know the main story and the context for their entrances and exits. Players who knew only their parts and a plot summary relied heavily on their cues and embedded stage directions to piece together information about what was going on, who they were addressing and who was going to respond.

The pressured system of rehearsal and performance was confusing for inexperienced actors, especially young ones, who were sometimes apprenticed to older actors while they were new to the workings of the stage. The apprentices, also known as boy actors, were usually aged between six or seven and thirteen or fourteen, and learned the art of acting from more established actors. Female roles were played by boy actors because women were not allowed to act on stage.

◆ Some of the activities throughout this book have asked you to look out for embedded stage directions. Look at these, or find some more, then discuss with a partner what a modern director might say to actors at these points. Are all of them necessary on a modern stage? Would you consider cutting some lines if they are not necessary? How should the actors perform the lines?

▼ An illustration from 1595 showing the Swan Theatre on Bankside in London. Wealthier people paid to sit in the levels that surrounded the stage on three sides.

Stage sets were limited in terms of scenery and lighting, so Shakespeare included detailed and often poetic descriptions of the time and place in various scenes. Audiences needed to use their imaginations to compensate for the bare stage! However, actors wore lavish costumes and a range of visual and sound effects were used to add spectacle to a performance. For example, animal organs may have been used on stage – including pigs' bladders filled with animal blood – during murder scenes. Cannonballs were rolled along tracks backstage to simulate thunder. Storm scenes such as the opening of *The Tempest*, or the scenes on the heath in *King Lear* and *Macbeth*, were probably accompanied by such sound effects. Bells, trumpets and drums were also used, as were a range of songs, background instrumental music and dance music.

A trapdoor on stage was also used in performances, allowing for such effects as a cauldron ascending with the Apparitions in *Macbeth*. The space above the stage, the upper structure known as the 'heavens', was decorated on the underside with stars and zodiac signs, and used for characters to descend and ascend during a performance.

Performance after Shakespeare

Since Shakespeare's time, *Macbeth* has always been popular. But like all of Shakespeare's plays, it has been rewritten, revised and adapted through the centuries, reflecting the tastes and the social and political circumstances of different times. Indeed, the playwright Thomas Middleton changed some of the Witches' scenes and further revised the play as early as 1610. It has been altered many times since then.

We might revere Shakespeare today, but writers, actors and audiences from earlier periods felt that his plays needed to be salvaged and rewritten. They 'improved' the perceived flaws in the plays and adapted them to suit the tastes of the day. Sir William Davenant (who claimed to be Shakespeare's illegitimate son) presented a radically changed version of *Macbeth* from that first published in the 1623 First Folio edition of all Shakespeare's plays. A record of this production in 1672 reads:

The Tragedy of Macbeth, *altered by Sir William Davenant; being dressed in all its finery, as new clothes, new scenes, machines, as flyings for the witches; with all the singing and dancing … being all excellently performed being in the nature of an opera.*

This version was published soon after the Civil War and, in new scenes, it asked the audience to consider the role of the monarchy. But the changes were so extensive that it could be argued that the play was no longer Shakespeare's at all, but rather something entirely new. Davenant cut the Porter and the Doctors, had Seyton change sides at the end, and altered the language so as not to offend his audience of gentry. Scenes were added: Lady Macbeth and Lady Macduff talked together; Macduff's role was greatly enlarged at the expense of Malcolm's; and the Witches turned up to support Macduff against Macbeth.

Davenant's version of the play remained the standard theatre script until the eighteenth century, when the actor David Garrick sought to stage a production of *Macbeth* 'as written by Shakespeare'. However, even Garrick could not resist the temptation of writing a long farewell speech for Macbeth, full of sorrow and self-condemnation. Some critics believe that Garrick's production, staged in 1744, marked a new phase in the play's performance history, a process of returning to the integrity and purity of the 1623 Folio script.

Successive actors and directors continued in this, and looked for new ways to explore Shakespeare's language, as well as to make each production relevant to the values of their society and culture. It seems that every society projects its own values on *Macbeth*. Even Davenant's now-derided version can be seen as a response to the growing interest in opera (it involved much music and dancing) and the political situation of the time.

From early in the twentieth century, the spectacular operatic effects were removed. Staging became simpler, partly in an attempt to return to the plainer values of Shakespeare's own stage. The creative tension between the script and the staging continued to mine rich new ways of imagining the play, and modern productions have radically reinterpreted and re-presented *Macbeth* in order to explore and stress different aspects of the play.

The Witches, in particular, have proved to be a source of inspiration for directors and actors. They have been presented as creations of Macbeth's mind and as puppet masters controlling each of the characters on stage. They have been shown as children, as a family unit of husband, wife and child, and as ugly old women. Other productions have portrayed them as sexually alluring young women, disruptive young men who merge with other characters, and even refuse collectors. They can be entertainers, dancers, roller-blading teenagers – anything that the director thinks articulates an aspect of the play that will further develop or frame key themes.

There is perhaps less freedom to experiment with the leading characters of Macbeth and Lady Macbeth, but again, both these parts have drawn radically different interpretations from some of the greatest actors of their age. Both characters challenge those playing the roles to decide whether to make them fully 'human', or to demonise them. Henry Irving's 1888 production was characterised by its dark, sombre atmosphere, and Irving played Macbeth as a liar and a murderer. In contrast, in this production Lady Macbeth was performed by the renowned Ellen Terry. She played the character as an 'enchanting being', free of malice, a doting wife who simply loved her husband (see the picture bottom right p. 169).

▼ **David Garrick in the title role during his 1744 performance of *Macbeth*. Lady Macbeth was played by Mrs Pritchard.**

Gradually, our understanding of the complexities of human behaviour developed, both through modern clinical medicine and, perhaps even more importantly, through the pioneering work done in the late nineteenth and early twentieth centuries by psychoanalysts such as Breuer, Freud (who wrote a brief study of Lady Macbeth) and Jung. As this understanding grew, artists became increasingly interested in the conscious and subconscious urges of individuals, and *Macbeth* lent itself very easily to interpretations that accentuated the inner lives of the main characters.

The relationship between Macbeth and his wife is fundamental to the play. Macbeth has wide-ranging relationships with almost all the other characters, but Lady Macbeth relates only to her husband. Actors have to decide how to play the relationship between these two characters as they grow estranged from each other.

A crucial aspect is how much they are in love, and some productions have presented their initial relationship as passionate and sensual. One famous remark about the production that starred Laurence Olivier and Vivien Leigh as the Macbeths was to remind audiences 'that Macbeth and his Lady were lovers before they were criminals'. Retaining both the light and darkness of each character – the love and criminality, so that one does not extinguish the other – is a challenge that will undoubtedly continue to interest actors and audiences in the future.

Other changes in society, including the rise of left-wing political parties and an increasingly radical feminism, saw productions focusing on areas of the script that emphasised certain political positions. For example, the feminist critic Janet Adelman claimed that Macbeth acts in the way he does because he is insecure about his own masculinity. Other feminist critics believe that the families represented in the play are essentially patriarchal, with children and wives largely absent or inconsequential. The only family we see that has a young (male) child is Macduff's, but his family is abandoned by the patriarch of the house, and then brutally murdered by the patriarch of Scotland.

Macbeth resonates with all societies, regardless of culture and time. An all-black adaptation of the play, *Umabatha*, has toured the world. It transformed *Macbeth* into a play about Zulu identity in early nineteenth-century South Africa. Chanting, drumming, and rhythmically beating shields, the huge cast created a tribal *Macbeth* of immense ritual power. The Zulu warriors grieved, rejoiced, welcomed and fought throughout their own unique re-staging of Shakespeare's tragedy.

The play has also been a rich source of inspiration for artists to reinterpret it in different forms. It has been made into opera, ballet, novels, movies, television programmes, songs, graphic texts, political cartoons and adverts. Now, in the age of the Internet, it has taken on a new life, as bloggers, amateur filmmakers and musicians adapt the text, perform it, and render it in new forms, spreading it to fresh and increasingly diverse audiences. *Macbeth*'s popularity can be explained in a number of ways: it has a relatively straightforward story, strong characters, powerful themes with universal appeal, and an economy of action that makes the plot unfold rapidly. And perhaps the key theme, ambition, resonates with everyone.

Whose *Macbeth* is it?

We tend to treat the script of *Macbeth* as something untouchable. As you will have seen in the various activities throughout this book, interpreting an episode in a particular way means focusing on certain aspects that we believe exist in the words. It is rare to see productions (other than those in translation) that change Shakespeare's language. But, as mentioned earlier, this has not always been the case.

◆ As a class, discuss how much freedom directors and actors should have in adapting *Macbeth*. Should every word remain untouched? Or is it permissible to cut scenes if they are not felt to be necessary (or if they are probably not by Shakespeare), such as the scene featuring Hecate? Is it right to make the play overtly political? Is it possible to keep the interpretation of the play separate from the society in which it is performed? Who judges such adaptations a success – the director, the cast, critics or the audience?

Macbeth on stage and on film

Macbeth is best experienced live, but if you are unable to see a production, or take part in one, there are many different film versions available for you to watch. Take time to find different versions of the text, but remember to view each one actively rather than passively. If you are analysing a movie adaptation of the play, think about:

- camerawork (angles, movement, shot type)
- sound (dialogue, sound effects, music)
- lighting (back light, key light)
- editing (simple cuts, montages, fade-out shots, dissolve cuts).

For each of these, consider what their effect is on the viewer, and how they add to (and sometimes detract from) the original script.

Write a review

Now try reviewing different versions of *Macbeth*. You could compare and contrast two movie versions, or two play productions. It might help to read film and theatre critics' reviews of past productions to get a sense of what they focus on and their depth of analysis. There are many very different interpretations of this play, so remain open-minded about each.

As you watch the productions, ask yourself what each is saying about its time and its culture. Above all, retain your own distinctive voice as you assess the qualities of the performances you watch.

Posters

Promotional posters provide a snapshot of a production. Their layout, typography and use of images convey the qualities of the movie or play as well as the period and culture in which it was devised.

◆ Look at the posters on these pages, then discuss in groups of three what key elements in *Macbeth* you think each production might highlight.

◆ Stay in your groups and design your own poster to promote a production of *Macbeth* that conveys the main values of a particular community. This community could be a school, an area of a town, a financial district or a whole society. Think carefully about the images and text you would include and why are they relevant to *Macbeth*.

THE W.P.A.
FEDERAL THEATRE NEGRO UNIT
MACBETH
BY WILLIAM SHAKESPEARE

Writing about Shakespeare

The play as text

Shakespeare's plays have always been studied as literary works – as words on a page that need clarification, appreciation and discussion. When you write about the plays, you will be asked to compose short pieces and also longer, more reflective pieces like controlled assessments, examination scripts and coursework – often in the form of essays on themes and/or imagery, character studies, analyses of the structure of the play and on stagecraft. Imagery, stagecraft and character are dealt with elsewhere in this edition. Here, we concentrate on themes and structure. You might find it helpful to look at the 'Write about it' boxes on the left-hand pages throughout the play.

Themes

It is often tempting to say that the theme of a play is a single idea, like 'death' in *Hamlet*, or 'the supernatural' in *Macbeth*, or 'love' in *Romeo and Juliet*. The problem with such a simple approach is that you will miss the complexity of the plays. In *Romeo and Juliet*, for example, the play is about the relationship between love, family loyalty and constraint; it is also about the relationship of youth to age and experience; and the relationship between Romeo and Juliet is also played out against a background of enmity between two families. Between each of these ideas or concepts there are tensions. The tensions are the main focus of attention for Shakespeare and the audience; this is also how the best drama operates – by the presentation of and resolution of tension.

Look back at the Themes boxes throughout the play to see if any of the activities there have given rise to information that you could use as a starting point for further writing about the themes of the specific play you are studying.

Structure

Most Shakespeare plays are in five acts, divided into scenes. These acts were not in the original scripts, but have been included in later editions to make the action more manageable, clearer and more like 'classical' structures. One way to get a sense of the structure of the whole play is to take a printed version (not this one!) and cut it up into scenes and acts, then display each scene and act, in sequence, on a wall, like this:

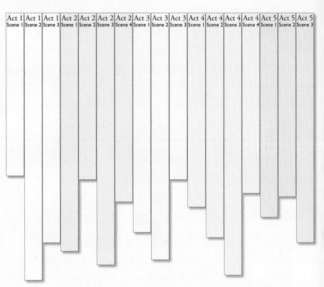

As you set out the whole play, you will be able to see the 'shape' of each act, the relative length of the scenes, and how the acts relate to each other (such as whether one act is shorter, and why that might be). You can annotate the text with comments, observations and questions. You can use a highlighter pen to mark the recurrence of certain words, images or metaphors to see at a glance where and how frequently they appear. You can also follow a particular character's progress through the play.

Such an overview of the play gives you critical perspective: you will be able to see how the parts fit together, to stand back from the play and assess its shape, and to focus on particular parts within the context of the whole. Your writing will reflect a greater awareness of the overall context as a result.

The play as script

There are different, but related, categories when we think of the play as a script for performance. These include *stagecraft* (discussed elsewhere in this edition and throughout the left-hand pages), *lighting*, *focus* (who are we looking at? Where is the attention of the audience?), *music and sound*, *props and costumes*, *casting*, *make-up*, *pace and rhythm*, and other *spatial relationships* (e.g. how actors move around the stage in relation to each other). If you are writing about stagecraft or performance, use the notes you have made as a result of the Stagecraft activities throughout this edition of the play, as well as any information you can find about the plays in performance.

What are the key points of dispute?

Shakespeare is brilliant at capturing a number of key points of dispute in each of his plays. These are the dramatic moments where he concentrates the focus of the audience on difficult (sometimes universal) problems that the characters are facing or embodying.

First, identify these key points in the play you are studying. You can do this as a class by brainstorming what you consider to be the key points in small groups, then debating the long-list as a whole class, and then coming up with a short-list of what the class thinks are the most significant. (This is a good opportunity for speaking and listening work.) They are likely to be places in the play where the action or reflection is at its most intense, and which capture the complexity of themes, character, structure and performance.

Second, drill down at one of the points of contention and tension. In other words, investigate the complexity of the problem that Shakespeare has presented. What is at stake? Why is it important? Is it a problem that can be resolved, or is it an insoluble one?

Key skills in writing about Shakespeare

Here are some suggestions to help you organise your notes and develop advanced writing skills when working on Shakespeare:

- Compose the title of your writing carefully to maximise your opportunities to be creative and critical about the play. Explore the key words in your title carefully. Decide which aspect of the play – or which combination of aspects – you are focusing on.
- Create a mind map of your ideas, making connections between them.
- If appropriate, arrange your ideas into a hierarchy that shows how some themes or features of the play are 'higher' than others and can incorporate other ideas.
- Sequence your ideas so that you have a plan for writing an essay, review, story – whichever genre you are using. You might like to think about whether to put your strongest points first, in the middle, or later.
- Collect key quotations (it might help to compile this list with a partner), which you can use as evidence to support your argument.
- Compose your first draft, embedding quotations in your text as you go along.
- Revise your draft in the light of your own critical reflections and/or those of others.

The following pages focus on writing about *Macbeth* in particular.

Writing about *Macbeth*

Any kind of writing about *Macbeth* will be informed by your responses to the play. Your understanding of how characters, plot, themes, language and stagecraft are all interrelated will contribute to your unique perspective. This section will help you locate key points of entry into the play so that your writing will be engaging and original. The best way to capture your reader's attention is to take them with you on a journey of discovering a new pathway into *Macbeth*.

But first, how do you find your unique perspective? You may want to start with a character – say, Lady Macbeth. From here, allow yourself to make free connections with the rest of the play. If you think about the development of her character throughout the play, and her relationship with Macbeth, you might reach the conclusion that in some ways she is similar to the Witches. Like them, Lady Macbeth is linked to evil, and she calls on familiar spirits to possess her. This may lead you to a consideration of how Shakespeare's representation of witches was influenced by historical events and people. You may also find yourself thinking about the way the play links evil and gender, and questions ideas of masculinity and femininity.

Lady Macbeth also tempts and torments Macbeth. This may lead you to consider the language she uses: is it similar to the Witches' language at any point in the play? Or does it create a menacing and tense atmosphere in a different way? You might want to compare the language Lady Macbeth uses at the beginning of the play with her broken, strained language at the end of the play.

You will need to refer to the poetic, linguistic and dramatic features of the language, and in order to do so, you will want to focus closely on some key speeches. These key speeches may draw your attention to one of two themes that open up more of your ideas about Lady Macbeth. For example, the theme of appearance and reality is a fruitful one for exploring her language and the way she displays a deception and manipulation similar to that of the Witches.

As you can see, your unique perspective of *Macbeth* will begin to develop as you think about what you are interested in, and allow yourself to make connections between the dramatic, contextual, linguistic and thematic features of the play. As you formulate your ideas into a coherent piece of writing, by using mind maps and essay plans, remember to refer back to the characters and events in the play, and to quote from the play to develop and extend your ideas further.

◆ Generate five of your own essay titles for writing about *Macbeth*. Try to compose your 'dream' questions that will give you plenty of scope to pull together all your ideas about the play and allow you to investigate new and interesting areas. These could be a mixture of creative and analytical: be as open-minded as possible. For example, you could start with 'Ambition, fate or bloodlust: what motivates the Macbeths to act in the way they do?'

◆ Once you have your five titles, work with a partner or in a small group to build up ten titles that are varied and clear, and that inspire you to actually write an essay in response.

Creative writing

At different times during your study of *Macbeth*, and during assessments and examinations, you will be writing about the play and your personal responses to it. Creative responses, such as those encouraged in the activities on the left-hand pages of this book, can allow you to be as imaginative as you want. This is your chance to develop your own voice and to be adventurous, as well as being sensitive to the words and images in the play. *Macbeth* is a rich, multi-layered text that benefits from many different approaches, both in performance and in writing. Don't be afraid of larger questions or implications that cannot be reduced to simple resolutions. The complex issues that have no easy answers are often the most interesting to write about.

Macbeth (the director's cut)

◆ Imagine that you are directing a movie version of *Macbeth*. As Shakespeare's shortest play, the producers want it to have additional scenes. In pairs, look at each act and think about where an extra scene could be used to develop key themes. Would you add a scene that explains what happened to the Macbeths' child? Or would you include Lady Macbeth's death scene? Now choose one and write it yourself in Shakespeare's language (using iambic pentameter if you can).

◆ As part of the promotional material, the characters are going to be interviewed so that they can explain their actions and give their views on the others. In pairs, write twenty questions that you would like to ask them. Then, in small groups, conduct the interviews and film them, if you can, so that the rest of the class can view them.

Essay

Some responses, such as essays, have a set structure and specific requirements. Writing an essay gives you a chance to explore your own interpretations, to use evidence that appeals to you, and to write with creativity and flair. It allows you to explore *Macbeth* from different points of view. You can approach the play from a number of critical perspectives or in relation to different themes. You will also need to explore the play in the social, literary, political and cultural contexts of its production (Shakespeare's day) and reception (today or at any point since Shakespeare's time).

An essay can be seen as an exploration of the play in which you chart a path to illuminate ideas that are significant to you. It is also an argument that uses evidence and structural requirements to persuade your readers that you have an important perspective on the play. You must integrate evidence from the script into your own writing by using embedded quotations – and by explaining the significance of each quotation and reference to the play. Some people like to remember the acronym PEA to help them here. P is the POINT you are making. E is the EVIDENCE you are taking from the script, whether it is a direct quotation, a summary of what is happening, or a reference to character, plot and themes. A is the ANALYSIS you give for using this evidence, which will reflect back on the point you are making and contain your personal response and original ideas.

◆ Put the following essay questions in order of difficulty (with number one being the most challenging) and discuss with others why you put them in that order. Choose a few to construct a detailed essay plan that reflects the advice given in these two pages.

1 Look at Act 1 Scene 3 of *Macbeth* and explore the ways in which Macbeth and Banquo are presented in this scene and elsewhere in the play.

2 'Macbeth is a plaything of the Witches: he has no free will and is therefore innocent of his crimes.' Discuss.

3 'The play is an analysis of male values; ultimately it sees masculinity as a destructive force.' To what extent do you agree with this statement?

4 Why is Act 2 Scene 1 so dramatically effective?

5 '*Macbeth* is an ancient text that has no relevance or parallels with my society.' How far do you agree with this assertion?

6 How does Macbeth change during the play?

7 Who is most responsible for Macbeth's fate?

8 Look at Act 3 Scene 4 of *Macbeth* and comment on how Macbeth and Lady Macbeth are presented in this scene and elsewhere in the play.

William Shakespeare
1564–1616

1564	Born Stratford-upon-Avon, eldest son of John and Mary Shakespeare.
1582	Marries Anne Hathaway of Shottery, near Stratford.
1583	Daughter Susanna born.
1585	Twins, son and daughter Hamnet and Judith, born.
1592	First mention of Shakespeare in London. Robert Greene, another playwright, described Shakespeare as 'an upstart crow beautified with our feathers'. Greene seems to have been jealous of Shakespeare. He mocked Shakespeare's name, calling him 'the only Shake-scene in a country' (presumably because Shakespeare was writing successful plays).
1595	Becomes a shareholder in The Lord Chamberlain's Men, an acting company that became extremely popular.
1596	Son, Hamnet, dies aged eleven.
	Father, John, granted arms (acknowledged as a gentleman).
1597	Buys New Place, the grandest house in Stratford.
1598	Acts in Ben Jonson's *Every Man in His Humour*.
1599	Globe Theatre opens on Bankside. Performances in the open air.
1601	Father, John, dies.
1603	James I grants Shakespeare's company a royal patent: The Lord Chamberlain's Men become The King's Men and play about twelve performances each year at court.
1607	Daughter Susanna marries Dr John Hall.
1608	Mother, Mary, dies.
1609	The King's Men begin performing indoors at Blackfriars Theatre.
1610	Probably returns from London to live in Stratford.
1616	Daughter Judith marries Thomas Quiney.
	Dies. Buried in Holy Trinity Church, Stratford-upon-Avon.

The plays and poems

(no one knows exactly when he wrote each play)

1589–95	*The Two Gentlemen of Verona, The Taming of the Shrew, First, Second* and *Third Parts* of *King Henry VI, Titus Andronicus, King Richard III, The Comedy of Errors, Love's Labour's Lost, A Midsummer Night's Dream, Romeo and Juliet, King Richard II* (and the long poems *Venus and Adonis* and *The Rape of Lucrece*).
1596–99	*King John, The Merchant of Venice, First* and *Second Parts* of *King Henry IV, The Merry Wives of Windsor, Much Ado About Nothing, King Henry V, Julius Caesar* (and probably the Sonnets).
1600–05	*As You Like It, Hamlet, Twelfth Night, Troilus and Cressida, Measure for Measure, Othello, All's Well That Ends Well, Timon of Athens, King Lear.*
1606–11	**Macbeth**, *Antony and Cleopatra, Pericles, Coriolanus, The Winter's Tale, Cymbeline, The Tempest.*
1613	*King Henry VIII, The Two Noble Kinsmen* (both probably with John Fletcher).
1623	Shakespeare's plays published as a collection (now called the First Folio).

Acknowledgements

Cambridge University Press would like to acknowledge the contributions made to this work by Rex Gibson.

Picture Credits

p. iii: Battersea Arts Centre 2000, © Donald Cooper/ Photostage; p. v: The Independent Players and New Vision Theatre 2011, © Charlie Neuman/ZUMA Press/Corbis; p. vi top: *Shogun Macbeth*, Pan Asian Repertory Theatre 2008, © Corky Lee; p. vi bottom: Out of Joint/Arcola Theatre 2004, © Donald Cooper/Photostage; p. vii top: Albery Theatre 2002, © Donald Cooper/Photostage; p. vii bottom: Albery Theatre 2002, © Donald Cooper/Photostage; p. viii top: West Yorkshire Playhouse 2007, © Donald Cooper/ Photostage; p. viii bottom: Ludlow Festival 2001, © Donald Cooper/Photostage; p. ix top: *The Kingdom of Desire*, The Contemporary Legend Theatre/Taiwan 1990, © Donald Cooper/Photostage; p. ix bottom: English Shakespeare Company/Peacock Theatre 1992, © Donald Cooper/ Photostage; p. x left: RSC/Royal Shakespeare Theatre 1996, © Donald Cooper/Photostage; p. x right: RSC/Royal Shakespeare Theatre 2004, © Donald Cooper/Photostage; p. xi left: RSC/Barbican Theatre 1983, © Donald Cooper/ Photostage; p. xi right: Out of Joint/Arcola Theatre 2004, © Donald Cooper/Photostage; p. xii top: Open Air Theatre 2007, © Donald Cooper/Photostage; p. xii bottom: Ludlow Festival 2001, © Donald Cooper/Photostage; p. 6: RSC/ Royal Shakespeare Theatre 1996, © Donald Cooper/ Photostage; p. 8 top left: Three witches of Belvoir woodcut 1600s, © Topfoto; p. 8 top right: © Gordon Anthony/Hulton Collection/Getty Images; p. 8 bottom left: Woodcut book illustration c. 1500, © Bettmann/Corbis; p. 8 bottom right: Battersea Arts Centre 2000, © Donald Cooper/Photostage; p. 10: Open Air Theatre 2007, © Elliott Franks/ArenaPAL; p. 14: RSC/Swan Theatre 2007, © Donald Cooper/ Photostage; p. 20: 'The Family of Henry VIII: An Allegory of the Tudor Succession' by Lucas de Heere c. 1572, © Getty Images; p. 22: Albery Theatre 2002, © Donald Cooper/ Photostage; p. 28: Shakespeare's Globe 2001, © Donald Cooper/Photostage; p. 30: Center for New Theater at CalArts/Almeida Theatre 2005; © Donald Cooper/

Photostage; p. 37 top: Schiller Theatre Company/Mermaid Theatre 1992, © Donald Cooper/Photostage; p. 37 bottom left: Minerva Theatre/Chichester Festival Theatre 2007 © Donald Cooper/Photostage; p. 37 bottom right: Ludlow Festival 2001, © Donald Cooper/Photostage; p. 44: RSC/ Swan Theatre 2007, © Donald Cooper/Photostage; p. 50: RSC/Royal Shakespeare Theatre 1996, © Donald Cooper/ Photostage; p. 54: Minerva Theatre/Chichester Festival Theatre 2007, © Donald Cooper/Photostage; p. 63 top left: Out of Joint/Arcola Theatre 2004, © Donald Cooper/ Photostage; p. 63 top right: Gielgud Theatre 2007, © AlamyCelebrity/Alamy; p. 63 bottom left: Ludlow Festival 2001, © Donald Cooper/Photostage; p. 63 bottom right: *Shogun Macbeth*, Pan Asian Repertory Theatre 2008, © Corky Lee; p. 64: RSC/Barbican Theatre 1989, © Donald Cooper/Photostage; p. 70: Ludlow Festival 2001, © Donald Cooper/Photostage; p. 74: Cheek by Jowl/Barbican Theatre 2010, © Robbie Jack/Corbis; p. 82: RSC/Royal Shakespeare Theatre 2004, © Stewart Hemley/RSC p. 86: The Royal Opera/Covent Garden 2002, © Donald Cooper/Photostage; p. 94: RSC/Royal Shakespeare Theatre 2004, © Donald Cooper/Photostage; p. 96: Cheek by Jowl/Barbican Theatre 2010, © Robbie Jack/Corbis; p. 97 top left: Bell Shakespeare/ Melbourne Arts Centre 2012, © Silas Brown; p. 97 top right: TR Warszawa/Edinburgh Festival 2012, © Robbie Jack/Corbis; p. 97 bottom: *Umabatha: The Zulu Macbeth*/Shakespeare's Globe Theatre 1997, © Donald Cooper/Photostage; p. 104: Opera North 2008, © Donald Cooper/Photostage; p. 108 left: West Yorkshire Playhouse 2007, © Donald Cooper/ Photostage; p. 108 right: RSC/Royal Shakespeare Theatre 2011, © Donald Cooper/Photostage; p. 110: RSC/Barbican Theatre 1993, © Donald Cooper/Photostage; p. 116: *The Kingdom of Desire*, The Contemporary Legend Theatre/ Taiwan 1990, © Donald Cooper/Photostage; p. 118: Leon Trotsky 1924, © Getty Images; p. 120: Out of Joint/Arcola Theatre 2004, © Geraint Lewis; p. 122: RSC 1999, © Geraint Lewis; p. 126: RSC/Royal Shakespeare Theatre 1996, © Donald Cooper/Photostage; p. 131 top: Out of Joint/Arcola Theatre 2004, © Geraint Lewis; p. 131 middle: RSC/Barbican Theatre 1983; © Donald Cooper/Photostage;

MACBETH

p. 131 bottom: RSC/Royal Shakespeare Theatre 2004, © Geraint Lewis; p. 134: 'Lady Macbeth Sleepwalking' by Henry Fuseli 1783, © Roger-Viollet/Topfoto; p. 136: Cheek by Jowl/Barbican Theatre 2010, © Geraint Lewis; p. 142: The Royal Opera/Covent Garden 2011, © Donald Cooper/ Photostage; p. 150: RSC/Barbican Theatre 1993, © Donald Cooper/Photostage; p. 154: 'The Death of Jezebel' by Gustave Doré, © Ann Ronan Picture Library/HIP/TopFoto; p. 159 top left: Battersea Arts Centre 2000, © Donald Cooper/ Photostage; p. 159 top right: The Royal Opera/Covent Garden 2002, © Donald Cooper/Photostage; p. 159 bottom: Salzburg Festival 2011, © Barbara Gindl/epa/Corbis; p. 161: Shakespeare's Globe 2010, © Donald Cooper/Photostage; p. 162: 'Henry Garnet Executed', © Mary Evans Picture Library/Alamy; p. 164: 'The Day of Judgement' illustration from the Guild Chapel, Stratford, by permission of the Shakespeare Birthplace Trust; p. 166 top: Cheek by Jowl/ Barbican Theatre 2010, © Geraint Lewis; p. 166 bottom: RSC/Barbican Theatre 1993, © Donald Cooper/Photostage;

p. 167: RSC/Royal Shakespeare Theatre 2004; © Donald Cooper/Photostage; p. 168: RSC/Swan Theatre 2007, © Geraint Lewis; p. 169 top: The Metropolitan Opera 2012, © Marty Sohl Photography; p. 169 bottom: 'Miss Ellen Terry as Lady Macbeth' by John Singer Sargent, © The Print Collector/Corbis; p. 171: Birmingham Repertory Theatre 1995, © Donald Cooper/Photostage; p. 174: 'The Long View of London from Bankside' by Wenceslaus Hollar; p. 175: Swan Theatre, Bankside, London c. 1595, Heritage Images/Corbis; p. 177: 'David Garrick and Mrs Pritchard in *Macbeth*' by Johann Zoffany 1768, © Topfoto; p. 178: Ninagawa Theatre Company/Lyttelton Theatre/ National Theatre 1987, © Donald Cooper/Photostage; p. 179: *Umabatha: The Zulu Macbeth*, Shakespeare's Globe Theatre 2001, © Adrian Dennis/epa/Corbis; p. 180: WPA Federal Theatre Negro Unit poster c. 1936, © Corbis; p. 181 top: Japanese film poster for *Throne of Blood* 1957, © TOHO/ The Kobal Collection; p. 181 bottom: Film poster 2006, © AF Archive/Alamy.

 Produced for Cambridge University Press by White-Thomson Publishing +44 (0)843 208 7460 www.wtpub.co.uk

Managing editor: Sonya Newland
Designer: Clare Nicholas
Concept design: Jackie Hill